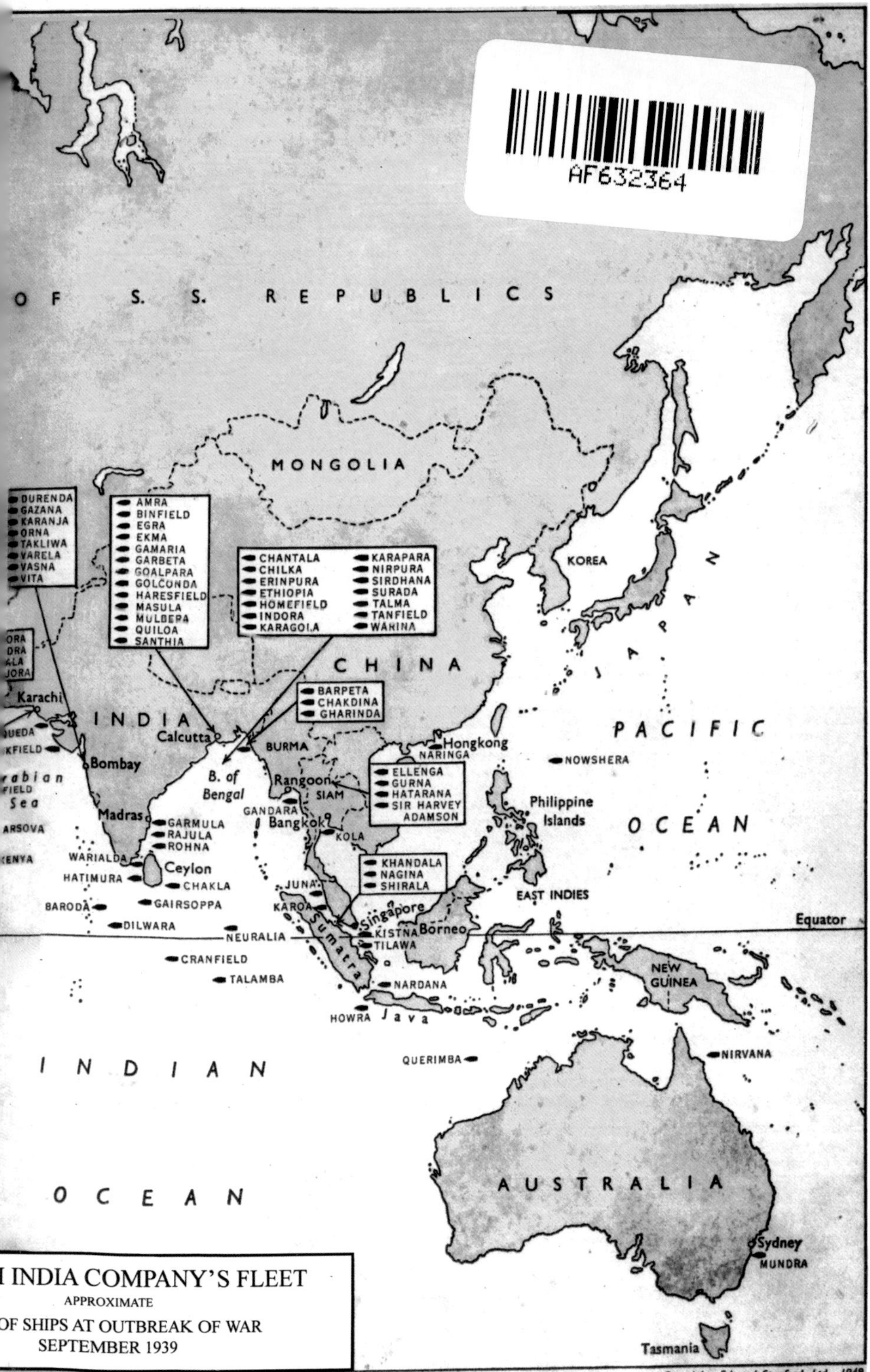

H INDIA COMPANY'S FLEET

APPROXIMATE

OF SHIPS AT OUTBREAK OF WAR

SEPTEMBER 1939

FOREWORD

By Sir William Crawford Currie, G.B.E.

That it should fall to me to have the privilege of writing a foreword to the story of the many parts played by the members—British and Indian alike—of the British India Steam Navigation Company in practically every quarter of the globe in the Second World War fills me with pride.

At the same time, I feel—and I am sure every reader will share this feeling—a deep sense of humility when I read of the feats of courage and endurance which the pages of this book unfold. They were displayed by our people at sea who, in addition to their own perilous situation, had to endure the knowledge that their wives and families at home were being subjected to the assault of air raids, flying bombs and V2 rockets. Well named is the title, beginning as it does with V, that famous sign with which a great Prime Minister encouraged the nation in the dark days of the early nineteen-forties.

The tale will, I hope, prove to be of some solace and pride to those who have been bereaved, a satisfaction to those who have survived and an inspiration to the young members of the Company who knew not the sea till after the war was over.

This book is dedicated to those who made the great sacrifice, whose memory let us salute with the proud words 'Semper Fidelis'.

ACKNOWLEDGEMENTS

The British India Company acknowledges with appreciation and thanks the many contributions made to this story by the Officers and Men of the Company's Fleet, and also the assistance rendered by the Ministry of Transport, without whose help it would have been difficult, if not impossible, to obtain much of the information.

Acknowledgement is also made to The Imperial War Museum for the plates facing page 30.

CONTENTS

PLATES

MAPS

1

THE FATE OF THE *GOGRA*

It may be that we cease; we cannot tell,
Even if we cease, life is a miracle.

Sonnet XXXVI—John Masefield

On the 26th March 1943, the s.s. *Gogra*, of 5,190 tons, Master—Captain John Drummond, sailed from the Clyde. She was a cargo vessel, fully laden, and as she passed down the river to the open sea, the crew could hear the ship's cat mewing far below in No. 4 hold. The cat had fallen into it and not been seen when the hatches were put on. There she lay, uninjured but unable to climb out, and thus condemned to three months' imprisonment until the cargo was discharged at Karachi. Her green eyes could be seen in the darkness twenty feet down the airshaft and her cries rent the hearts of the crew. They took counsel and presently arranged for a supply of food to be lowered to the cat, which was soon receiving a small tray of fish and milk at regular intervals. The cat became used to the system of feeding, but no persuasion would make it sit on the tray and be hauled to safety.

The following day, the *Gogra* took position No. 111 in a convoy off the Isle of Islay, and on the day after that found herself leading ship of the eleventh, the outside starboard, column. The escort was composed of one sloop-of-war, H.M.S. *Black Swan*, and seven corvettes. All went well until about 9 p.m. on 2nd April. At that time 'there prevailed a fresh easterly wind and a cloudy sky, with moderate sea and swell, the night being pitch black, with no moon or stars'. In accordance with orders, the s.s. *Gogra* altered course twenty degrees to port. The officer of the watch, Extra Chief Officer G. R. Mudford, left the navigation for the flying bridge to adjust the new course, and had just given the helmsman his final order, 'Steady', when a shock shook the ship from stem to stern and the binnacle light was extinguished. The darkness was but momentary and was broken by 'a tremendous white flash which extended in an arc from bow to stern . . . and was as high as our mast'. Mudford found himself on his knees, his arms round the compass, the target for 'a shower of water and pieces of metal'. Getting to his feet he ran to the navigating bridge, pausing only to pick up his lifebelt from the chartroom settee. Ordering the Seacunny (Indian Quartermaster) away from the wheel, he tried to stop the engines but the telegraph was jammed. As he switched on the alarm bells he began to feel the ship sink beneath him. From the time of the explosion to her disappearance below the surface, no more, he thought, than twenty seconds elapsed. What happened next can be told in his own words.

'I went down inside the bridge for many fathoms, feeling the water forcing into my lungs in spite of doing all I could to resist it. Then I felt myself somersaulting upwards for what seemed a long time and I felt the pressure on nostrils and ears decreasing, but not before I had to take a short breath of water. I broke surface, shooting a few feet into the air, and found myself floating in a mass of small wood with a case alongside me which had a batten across it just right for me to grip. I had no lifebelt, as I had had no time to put it on after getting it from the chart room. Everything floating was whirling round, which continued for a long time, with a very sickening effect on me. There were, I think, about fifteen men afloat, many with lifebelts and lights working perfectly; also I suspect there were many empty lifebelts whose owners did not get them on in time. The Engineers' messroom boy was close behind me, and grabbed me around my neck. His head was high out of the water, and his lifebelt and light in good order. I told him to let me go and to hold the case as I was doing, which he immediately did and stayed quiet.

'These men with me were shouting for help and blowing their whistles vigorously for about twenty minutes, but I think the majority died of cold within half an hour, as there was no sound from them after that. The messroom boy alongside me kept letting himself slacken up, and three times I pulled him straight and held his head up, but he died in half an hour. I tied him to my arm and kept him near me so that his light illuminated me, and I tried unsuccessfully to take off my bridge coat so as to lighten myself, with a view to taking off the dead man's lifebelt and using it, but it was impossible to get the lifebelt off without the risk of losing the case supporting me, so I gave up the attempt and continued treading water after kicking off my knee-boots.

'I collected some small pieces of wood together and held them in a bundle under my left arm; they gave good support as long as I held on to the case with my right hand.

'After about forty minutes in the water, I looked around and saw behind me a ship, slowly closing, like a pair of shears. The two ends met and she sank. That was the first I knew of there being other victims of attack than the *Gogra.*

'The convoy had gone on, and it seemed to me I was alone. I stayed still for some time, then made one or two efforts to lie over the case so as to get a little support, but the case was too small to hold me, and capsized me, so I gave that up. I stayed quiet then until soon after midnight, feeling so bitterly cold that I thought I could not last much longer. I shivered so violently at times that I temporarily lost my bundle of wood from under my arm. Cramp was starting in my legs.

'Then a corvette came out of the darkness straight for me, firing into the water just over me, and passed me about a hundred feet away. I called as loudly as I could; someone answered, she steamed away, my timber disintegrated, the case revolved, and I made a supreme effort and retrieved it. Then the corvette returned, lowered a boat and picked me up, three hours and twenty minutes after the sinking. I lay in the boat and listened while the crew rowed around examining bodies, but there was nobody else alive to be picked up.'

Mudford was put to bed in the sick-bay and learnt the next morning that his rescue had been a matter of singular good fortune, for the light on the dead messroom boy's life-jacket had been thought by the Captain of the corvette, a Free French officer named La Malouine, to be a trick of the U-boat and he had set his ship to ram her. Just before reaching the light the mistake had been realized, and the ship had altered course. The man on her deck had heard Mudford shouting and thus he was picked up.

On rejoining the convoy Mudford was trans-shipped to the *Black Swan* and was kept under medical treatment till the safe arrival of that ship with the others at Freetown on 14th April.

The *Gogra* had not been the only victim. The ship which

Mudford had seen folding up like a pair of shears was the *Katha* of the Henderson Line, following astern of the *Gogra*. But the enemy U-boat paid the penalty for a daring and successful attack. She had lain on the surface ahead of the convoy and waited until the ships of which it was composed were all round her. In the darkness of the night, the corvettes had not seen her, nor could she be heard, for her engines were not running. As the *Gogra* came into her sights, she fired, and repeated the attack on the *Katha*. By that time, however, the *Black Swan*, realizing what had happened, had turned and made straight for the submarine, which crash dived too late. The depth charges went down, and the U-boat joined her victims on the bottom.

Arrived at Freetown, Mudford found that there were thirty-seven other survivors from the *Gogra*, three of them being Indians. His stay was short. Two days after landing —he had spent them in a native hut where an old negress cooked the meals on a spit over a fire burning in a hole dug in the ground—Mudford boarded the *Queen Mary* and a week later was home again 'in bed at Highgate with a kit-bag full of fruit and chocolate'.

The *Gogra* was one of fifty-one ships belonging to the British India Steam Navigation Company which were sunk during the Second World War. How they came by their fate and how their more fortunate sisters maintained the great tradition of the British Merchant Navy must now be recounted.

But, first, what of the Company? How was it founded and by whom? What are its traditions and its claims to have been of service at the hour of peril and honour?

2

THE BRITISH INDIA STEAM NAVIGATION COMPANY

All in the feathered palm tree tops
the bright green parrots screech,
The white line of the running surf
goes booming down the beach.

Harbour Bar—John Masefield

On the 27th March 1854, both Houses of Parliament were made acquainted by the Queen that their country was at war with Russia, but some months were to pass before her subjects first heard the name of Florence Nightingale. That autumn Her Majesty went, as her custom was, to Balmoral for her annual holiday, where she indulged in 'the usual walks, rides, boatings and sketchings', while Prince Albert went deerstalking. Mr. Moses Moses was sentenced to be transported for fourteen years for keeping what was described as a depot for the reception of stolen goods 'of a magnitude which has no parallel'; a clergyman, the Reverend Thomas Robinson, committed suicide by flinging himself from the summit of Shakespeare Cliff; Napoleon III fought a 'grand mimic battle' between Boulogne and Calais, in which 'the Emperor was of course victorious'; Mr. Gulles Andover won the Derby stakes, Indian Stocks fluctuated between 231 and 241, and the Light Brigade charged the Russian guns at Balaclava.

The year 1854 was, it will be perceived, typical of the reign of private enterprise, still in its vigorous, all conquering youth. The power of the middle classes, its prophets, priests and kings, was growing steadily and sturdily. It was a stable, if expanding world. There was no need to wait for opportunity to knock on the door; it could be found at the end of the street, or certainly across one of the Seven Seas, then under the absolute dominion of the British Navy.

Yet change was in the air. Steam was everywhere beginning to take the place of sail. Even in the Far East where the tempo of progress was slower, a steamship, the *Enterprise*, had been displaying in the Indian Ocean the advantages of the new form of locomotion for the best part of thirty years. Other vessels followed her, until by 1854 the East India Company had at last become convinced that a regular service of steam vessels between India and Burma for the carriage of mails and passengers was highly desirable.

Opportunity was there waiting, and it was grasped with both hands by Mr. William Mackinnon, a young Scot from Campbeltown, who had been employed for several years by a firm of foreign merchants in Glasgow. In their service he had acquired that experience of business which was to have so decisive an influence upon his subsequent career. So well did he justify the high opinion formed of him by his employer, that, some three years after he became an assistant, Mackinnon was offered a partnership, which he would probably have accepted but for the invitation of an old Campbeltown friend to join him as a working partner in his business in India. The friend was Mr. Robert Mackenzie who had sought his fortune in that land some years before and established a general store in one of the smaller towns on the Ganges. In 1847 Mackinnon went out to India, and for eight years Mackenzie and he in partnership pursued the business so successfully that in 1851 they were able to transfer their headquarters to Calcutta.

Mackenzie, the older man, possessed the same qualities as Mackinnon, and in addition a number of friends in India and Scotland who were ready to risk their money in a new enterprise. With their financial support Mackenzie and Mackinnon decided to become shipowners and formed in 1854 the Burmah Steam Navigation Company. Their first steamer, the *Cape of Good Hope*, of 700 tons, was followed by the *Baltic*, of similar tonnage, and these vessels maintained a fortnightly service between Calcutta, Akyab, Rangoon and Moulmein. The start was propitious, but the company's operations were brought to an abrupt, though temporary, close in 1857 when its vessels were hastily ordered by the Government to carry reinforcements to India. It was the year of the Mutiny and business was at a standstill; but the Company rendered its first special service to Britain by transporting from Ceylon to Calcutta the old 35th Regiment of Foot, the first reinforcements to reach the hard-pressed Government troops.

In 1858, when the danger was over, the Company's business expanded and a third ship, the *Burma*, of 900 tons, was added to the small fleet. All was well again, and in 1862 when the Company secured a new Mail Contract, the British India Steam Navigation Company was erected on the foundations of the pioneer Company. Almost immediately a series of misfortunes befell the two pioneers which might have wrecked the enterprise of less resolute men. The *Cape of Good Hope* was run down in the Hooghly by a steamer belonging to the young Peninsular and Oriental Line, and a new vessel, the *Calcutta*, was wrecked on the Witlow bank fifteen hours after leaving the Clyde on her maiden voyage. Bankruptcy, that most dreaded of Victorian spectres, loomed menacingly above the brown office buildings and dusty palm trees of Calcutta.

Undaunted, Mackinnon raised fresh capital in England and, refusing to contract, instead expanded the service so that by 1863 the Company's fleet numbered seventeen, and regular voyages were being made from Calcutta to Singapore, Chittagong, the Andaman Isles, Madras, Bombay, Karachi, and even as far as the torrid ports of the Persian Gulf.

To the financial risks taken by pursuing this policy of expansion, physical were sometimes added. Piracy was far from unknown in the Malay Archipelago and the ships of the Company were not always safe even in the Shat el Arab. In the summer of 1872, for example, the s.s. *Cashmere*, lying at anchor just below the town of Basrah, was attacked by a band of Arabs disguised as passengers, who carried out 'their bloody work with expedition and success'. They removed £50,000 and plundered the passengers, killing those who resisted and severely wounding the Chief Officer. Forty of them were subsequently captured and half of them hanged on gibbets beside the scene of their crime.

The importance of this bold policy of expansion is difficult to over-estimate. At that time Anglo-Indian trade was congested and the means of transport uncertain and precarious. The steamships of the Company soon changed this situation and the contract concluded with the Government of India, under the impulse of the far-sighted Sir Bartle Frere, had far-reaching conclusions. By its terms the Government could, and did, transport troops more quickly and more cheaply than ever before and the trading houses of India were served with an efficiency on a scale up till then unknown. The Company's ships, propelled as they were by steam, were able to reach ports which had hitherto been regarded as unapproachable during the stormy monsoon period. Further away, on the other side of the Indian Ocean, more trade began to flow through the pirate-haunted waters of the Malay Straits. The years immediately following the Indian Mutiny were ones of high endeavour, bold expansion and hardy pioneering. The sun of prosperity, glimpsed by Mackinnon low down on the Eastern horizon, was now climbing towards the zenith, when in 1869 a new and dark cloud obscured its face.

The Suez Canal was opened. The old 'Overland Route' which had carried so much merchandise to and from India, much of it taken still further afield by the Company's ships, was changed for its operators in a few months from an asset into a liability. Ships of all kinds, many of them powered with new and much more economical compound engines, entered into competition with the British India Steam Navigation Company. The reaction of the Directors was immediate and bold. Their ships were sent westwards one by one for a complete re-fit in the Clyde. New and larger vessels were built and by 1889 a new contract had been obtained, this time from the Portuguese Government, so that the Company's vessels began to call at Lisbon and were soon running between London, Mombasa and Zanzibar.

The most romantic phase of William Mackinnon's career began in 1872 when he played a leading part in opening regular trade with the East Coast of Africa. Perceiving the high importance to Great Britain of a permanent connection with East Africa, and the prospect of high profits for his own Company, he put British India steamers on to regular trade runs between India and Zanzibar and linked the India-bound steamers at Aden with vessels reaching Zanzibar from that port. So satisfied was the Sultan Barghash with the benefits accruing to his dominions from the new Line, and so greatly was he impressed by the integrity and the capacity of Mackinnon, that in 1877 he made him a very remarkable offer. He was ready, he affirmed, to grant 'a concession for seventy years of the customs and the administration of the dominions of Zanzibar, including all rights of sovereignty' excepting only certain minor reservations with regard to the islands of Zanzibar and Pemba. At this point the Foreign Office intervened and so determined was its disapproval that Mackinnon was constrained to proceed no further with this advantageous transaction.

A few years later, another service was instituted and the Company was presently linking London with Colombo and on to Brisbane through the Torres Straits. Thus, less than a generation after it had been founded, the network of its services was spread wide over the Far East, with tentacles running up to Tilbury.

Three years before the contract with the Portuguese Government had been concluded, another Scotsman, of the same fine breed as that of Mackinnon, reached Calcutta. James Lyle Mackay, before he died to be created Earl Inchcape of Strathnaver for his services, joined the Company as a clerk. At first he seemed in no way remarkable, but one day a sudden decision involving large sums had to be taken. It was taken by young Mackay in the absence of the Calcutta Manager, who was in Poona, and, as a result, the firm was saved serious loss. After this, Mackay was a marked man. Promotion came quickly. He was taken into partnership and presently himself became senior partner in Calcutta. His energy was as great as his acumen, and when he died, in 1932, the Company, of which he was chairman, owned 123 cargo and passenger vessels of a total aggregate of 726,089 tons.

The last twenty years of the nineteenth century witnessed a continuous expansion of activity, beginning with the mail service from London to Brisbane already mentioned. It was inaugurated on Saturday, 12th February 1881, when the s.s. *Merkara* left the Victoria Docks under the command of Captain J. J. Ballantyne. The start was not propitious, for the majority of the Lascars went sick 'with different ailments' which the ship's doctor discovered were all due to the excessive cold, the winter being one of the most severe of that century. In the Bay of Biscay 'the union screw connecting the steel rope running from the steam steering gear for'ard to the rudder quadrant' broke, and the vessel rolled 'helpless in the trough of the sea', for an hour till engineers could repair it. After this contretemps all went well until the *Merkara* reached Keppel Bay where the Lascar butler died and was buried at sea, with some difficulty as he weighed 'nothing under twenty stone'. Eventually the ship docked safely on 12th April and the new service had begun.

Expansion still continued. The South African war broke out, and it was in steamers belonging to the British India Company that the Indian contingent arrived to take its share in the fighting. Altogether thirty-seven steamers were engaged on transport service during that war and in the China Expedition of 1900–01, thirty-nine. By then the Company was well used to carrying troops. Stumbling up her gangways in the footsteps of the old 35th Regiment of Foot had come first the troops that had fought in the Abyssinian war of 1857–63, then those of the Russo-Turkish war of 1878, the Zulu war in 1879, the Transvaal war of 1881, the Suakin expedition of 1885, the Persian expedition of 1888, the Uganda Rising of 1897, the Sudan war and the expedition for the occupation of Crete in 1898.

Fifteen years went by, and in 1914 another and larger

conflict, the First World War, broke out. At once a great shortage of vessels ploughing along the coast of India and between that country and Britain occurred, and at different times during the four years the war lasted, as many as 120 vessels of the Company were on Government service, carrying troops, stores and animals, or acting as hospital ships or even as armed cruisers. Twenty-one of the Company's steamers were sunk by enemy action, with heavy losses among officers and Indian seamen.

From 1917 to 1919 India was threatened by one of her periodic famines and the Company was called upon to provide all the necessary tonnage for the transportation of foodstuffs from Burma to India.

Then, as in the years which immediately followed the opening of the Suez Canal, the Company found itself once more facing competition. This time it came not from the West but from the East, from the country which it had served so well for more than sixty years. The spirit of nationalism was developing in India and this, mingled with a not unnatural desire to take advantage of the high rates for freight then prevailing, led to the formation of a number of rival shipping companies, of which the most important was the Scindia, which acquired six vessels in 1922. By that year, however, shipping rates all over the world were beginning to fall and profits to become smaller. It would doubtless have been possible for the British India Company, with its far larger fleet and wider connections, to have fought and successfully destroyed its rivals. Instead, however, it preferred to negotiate an amicable arrangement with them, and to that end concluded a ten year agreement under which the vessels of the Scindia Company confined their trade to that of carrying cargo within certain areas. In return they were allowed to double their fleet and a series of further agreements extended the co-operation between the two Companies up to 1939.

The Company had in 1914, under the stress of the First World War, become fused with the P. & O. Company. In December of that year Sir Thomas Sutherland retired from the chairmanship of the second, and the two Companies placed themselves under the able chairmanship of Lord Inchcape. Subsequently the New Zealand Shipping Company, the Federal Line, the Union Steamship Company of New Zealand, the Nourse Line, the Hain Line, and the General Steam Navigation Company joined the group, which presently comprised no less than two and a half million tons of shipping.

Despite the slump and the difficulties of the years between the two wars, constant improvements were made in the vessels of all these Companies, and special attention was paid by the British India Company to its troopships. They were handsome vessels, their beauty well set off by their white hulls, with a bright blue band along their entire length, and yellow funnels. When not carrying troops, they were used on pleasure cruises, in which, among other classes of passengers, large numbers of schoolboys were carried, mainly to Baltic ports. In contrast to the yellow funnels of the troopers were those of the other ships of the Company which were painted black with two white bands. Both were for years, and are again, 'the most familiar sight on the world's great trade routes in the East. From London through the Mediterranean, the Suez Canal and down the East Coast of Africa to Durban; on the coast of India; up the Persian Gulf; throughout the Indian Ocean; in and around the ports of the Straits Settlements; along the coasts of China and Japan; south to Australia.'

Contrary to the hopes of the world, the war of 1914–18

brought no promise of lasting peace. We had scotched the snake, not killed it, and soon the prospect of another and a fiercer struggle became visibie to those with eyes to see. As early as 1931 the Director of Sea Transport of the Admiralty approached the Company with a request that four of its passenger vessels 'should be earmarked for special Naval service in a national emergency'. The assurance was immediately given. In 1935, with the prospect of war against Italy, in support of the policy of sanctions laid upon her by the League of Nations as the result of her invasion of Abyssinia, the Company was asked what vessels it could place at the disposal of the Admiralty between the 1st and 8th October. Six passenger and three cargo vessels were immediately allocated, and in the following year the chairman renewed the Company's undertaking that in an emergency the whole of its fleet would be placed at the disposal of His Majesty's Government. Less than three years passed and this promise had to be fulfilled.

It is with the adventures of the vessels and the gallant crews which sailed in them in fulfilment of this promise that this book is concerned. A spirit of enterprise and service had inspired the Company from the beginning and had made them the owners of the biggest merchant fleet in the Empire. Already during the First World War it had had an opportunity to display itself. Now, with Germany once more determined to achieve or lose all by the arbitrament of the sword, it was to be displayed in an heroic degree.

3

THE FIRST TWENTY-SEVEN MONTHS

3rd September 1939 *to 7th December* 1941

Man with his burning soul
Has but an hour of breath
To build a ship of truth
In which his soul may sail.

Truth—JOHN MASEFIELD

On the 3rd September 1939, the British India Steam Navigation Company was still operating most of its vessels as a commercial undertaking concerned with trade in Far Eastern waters. Its regular services from Calcutta included among others the weekly service as far as Singapore and fortnightly to Japan; a monthly service to Australia; three or four sailings monthly to Bombay and Karachi; while Rangoon and Madras, Singapore and Bangkok, were linked weekly. The Persian Gulf was served three times a week from Bombay. Altogether, twenty-two regular services were in operation. Its ships engaged upon these and other voyages were spread far and wide; twenty-three in Calcutta, nine in Bombay, ten in Rangoon, two in Liverpool and the remainder spread out along the Kathiawar, the East African, the Malabar and the Arakan coasts, the Bay of Bengal, the Indian Ocean, the Persian Gulf, the Atlantic and in Australian waters. All were soon to be concerned in playing each her part in a struggle which, though it began with deceptive mildness, would certainly to discerning eyes develop into a mortal conflict.

Their adventures varied according to the nature and type of work they were called upon to do. Some ships, the greater number, continued under the general control of the Ministry of War Transport to carry passengers and cargo as in the days of peace, though the nature and quantity of both were changed. Others were taken over by the Royal Navy, save for two which found themselves in the service of the Royal Air Force. Yet others were converted into hospital ships. Finally there were those which became troopships. The process of taking over the Company's ships was on the whole rapid, and by Easter 1940, the whole fleet was under the orders of either the Admiralty or the Ministry of War Transport.

The first to come into contact with the war was the s.s. *Barpeta*, later taken over by the Military Stores Service, and she did so, curiously enough, far from the scene of battle in the ardent waters of the Persian Gulf. She was a small passenger vessel, and, on 10th September 1939, she was moving up the Gulf towards the port of Muscat, when her Master, Captain W. F. Putt, received a signal from the Senior Naval Officer, Bombay, stating that an aircraft of the Royal Air Force on its way to Karachi was down somewhere in the desert near the Gulf and asking that he should try to rescue its crew. Captain Putt was not very hopeful, but he altered course and steamed for eighty miles as close to the Persian coast-line as he could safely take his ship. Anchoring for the night in a large bay, he sent up rockets, and when dawn came dispatched a lifeboat to the shore, in charge of the Chief Officer. Returning in the afternoon, he reported that the surf was too high to make a landing possible, but, in the meantime, a light had been seen flashing from the barren and desolate interior. At dusk the Master was able to establish communication by means of a signalling lamp with those who had displayed the light. They reported that they were the crew of the missing aircraft, four in number of whom two were injured, and that their aircraft was broken beyond repair. They were told to go down to the beach if they could and at daylight the lifeboat went out again, this time with a doctor and the Third Officer on board. Anchoring with difficulty just outside the surf, the Third Officer and two Indians swam ashore with a line and the crew of the aircraft were one by one hauled through the surf to the lifeboat. The next day they were landed at Muscat, having been taken from a country which 'was all sand with no fresh water'. The Third Officer and the two Indians received the Albert Medal, the Master a gold cigarette case from the RAF and a threat of gaol from an 'enraged' Persian Governor who some time later discovered that they had violated Persian territorial waters in order to carry out this rescue.

Two months later, another of the Company's vessels, the s.s. *Sirdhana*, received a sharper reminder that the Empire was at war. On 13th November she sailed from Singapore harbour carrying a number of deported Chinese, whose presence in that port was not considered desirable by the authorities. Arrived off the Raffles Hotel, she struck a mine, one of those in a newly-sown field, and sank half a mile from shore. The next casualty was not due to enemy action. On 24th February 1940 the s.s. *Golconda* went aground in the Karnafuli River near Chittagong and took no further part in the war.

The First Twenty-seven Months

The year which was to see the fall of Denmark, Norway, Holland, Belgium and France opened quietly enough on land and in the air. The troops in Northern France remained at their posts in contact with the enemy, but made no effort to attack them. Save for a half-hearted raid on the Firth of Forth and some scattered combats over France, the Luftwaffe remained quiescent, while Bomber Command showered leaflets on the enemy and sought without success to fulfil an odd injunction, that when seeking to destroy the German Fleet they should take the greatest care 'not to injure the civilian population'. At sea, however, matters were different. From the beginning quarter had been neither asked nor given. The attacks on our merchant ships, which had opened with the torpedoing of the *Athenia* within a few hours of the outbreak of war, were pressed with great persistence. To those by torpedo from U-boats were added attacks made by bombs from aircraft. One of the Company's ships, the M.V. *Domala*, the first of its fleet to be driven by Diesel engines, was on her way from Antwerp to Southampton, carrying a number of Indian seamen, most of whom had been serving on board German merchant-ships and had been released by the Germans to enable them to return to India. At about five o'clock in the morning of 2nd March 1940, in the light of a waning moon, the ship was proceeding down channel when the look-outs observed an aircraft flying towards St. Catherine's Point. As she approached the ship she shewed her lights and this was taken as a signal that she belonged to the Royal Air Force. 'No special notice was therefore taken of her, neither was the anti-aircraft gun brought into action.' The aircraft swung round, flew low over the ship and dropped one or several bombs; accounts differ. It, or they, fell upon a vital spot, penetrating to the engine-room and there bursting. In a moment the superstructure and cabins of the ship were enveloped in flames, and the fire raged so fiercely as to be immediately out of control. The Fourth Officer, Maclean, was blown overboard by the blast. Captain Fitt gave orders for the ship to be abandoned and the boats to be got away as quickly as possible. He himself remained on the bridge and was never seen again. He was probably killed by a second stick of bombs dropped by the hostile aircraft. A strong wind was blowing and there was a heavy sea. This made the work of lowering the boats exceedingly difficult, nor was the situation improved by the German bomber which flew up and down machine-gunning all who were seeking to escape. Several were killed by bullets when clinging to rafts in the sea. A destroyer in the offing came to the rescue and picked up a number of survivors from the boats and from the water. She tried to come under the *Domala's* stern to enable those still on board to jump down upon her decks, but the heavy seas prevented these manoeuvres. The Dutch ship, the *Jonge Willem*, in the neighbourhood, also picked up some fifty survivors and by so doing attracted the unwelcome attentions of the Heinkel 111, which repeatedly attacked her with machine-gun fire, and dropped a bomb twenty feet from her quarter, but there were no casualties. A few more were rescued by lifeboats which were put out from the shore. Despite this savage attack, which it may be remembered was the first made by air on a ship, there was no panic. On the contrary, the demeanour of those on board shewed courage of a high order. Among them was Junior Engineer J. Dunn, of Kelty, in Fife. The explosion of the bomb broke his leg and the fire severely burned his face. Refusing to be helped, he crawled the length of the deck, and climbed a forty-foot perpendicular iron ladder on to the poop. Thence, equipped with a lifebelt, he was lowered into the sea and picked up, only to die of his wounds. 'He was the bravest man in the ship,' reported the

M.S. DOMALA
Damage by bombs March 1940

Chief Officer, W. Brawn. Cadet Duval was one of five cadets making their first voyage. He leapt overboard with the rest and found himself clinging to a raft with other men, who 'were compelled to let go owing to exhaustion and exposure'. He held on and was picked up unconscious. When making his report on the attack he added: 'As soon as I am fit I hope to be off to sea again.'

Out of the 143 passengers and 148 British and Indian crew, 108 were lost, and a few more died from the effects of exposure in ice-cold water. The *Domala*, still on fire, was taken in tow and brought into harbour, where she was subsequently reconstructed and served the Ministry of War Transport. Her repair was made the subject of a peremptory minute by the First Lord of the Admiralty, Mr. Churchill, who urged that she should be 'seized upon and repaired in the plainest way for the roughest work.' The attack upon her raised the greatest indignation. Questions were asked in Parliament and the Press reported it in detail. To many, lulled into a false sense of security by the inaction of the 'twilight war', it seemed an ominous foretaste of what was to come. It was.

Six weeks after the attack on the *Domala*, Hitler shewed his hand. Denmark and Norway were invaded and a month later the tide of war, sweeping southwards, flooded across Holland, Belgium and France. Those were desperate days, and when France collapsed and sued for an armistice on 17th June, the end seemed near. On that day, the s.s. *Madura* (Captain J. L. Beatty), one of the Company's passenger ships with accommodation for about 190, found herself close to the war. Since its outbreak, save for one voyage when she had brought to England from Gibraltar a shipload of women and children, she had been on the East African run; but now, being suddenly diverted, the *Madura* put into Bordeaux, where she was soon to find her accommodation stretched to the utmost. In addition to her normal complement of passengers, she took on board 1,300 refugees, the great majority being British subjects, resident in Belgium and France, who had fled to that port before the advent of the German armies. Most were penniless, some distinguished. Among them was Sir Maurice Peterson, the retiring British Ambassador from Madrid, M. Pierre Cot, Mr. Henri Bernstein, the dramatist, Mr. Osuski, the Czechoslovak Minister in Paris, Mlle Eve Curie, and a number of well known British journalists. The *Madura's* crew rose to the occasion. The stewards and chefs worked night and day, meals were organized in shifts and were eaten with scarcely a pause from dawn to dusk. The ship's baker, one Forsythe, was 'a hefty Huddersfield man'. He had need to be, for he had but one oven and this he kept more or less constantly at work to provide bread, which was the main article of diet.

The *Madura* was well found, but an increase of 1,300 souls in her passenger list strained her resources to the utmost, and when she reached Falmouth forty-eight hours after leaving Bordeaux, they were entirely exhausted. For the most part, the refugees were both astonished and grateful at the 'sheer generosity' shewn towards them by *Madura's* crew. 'No one,' records Richard Capell of the *Daily Telegraph*, 'was asked for his papers any more than if he had been escaping from a burning house. There was no distinction shewn between the British and the foreigners. . . . Now and then a comic note was struck as when certain passengers, accustomed to luxury cruises, gave haughty orders to the Marines on board.' 'The appearance of the public rooms,' reported Mr. H. W. Cooper, the Purser, 'resembled the London tube air-raid shelters, for there were all sorts and conditions of men, women and children sleeping huddled up together with not an inch of space to spare.' Of these not a few were French, and when the radio sets on board, tuned into Bordeaux, announced the surrender of France, 'they all had tears streaming down their faces and the ship resounded to moans.'

The next incident of note in which one of the Company's cargo ships was involved occurred on 18th November 1940, when Mr. Bellew, the fifth engineer of the s.s. *Nowshera*, plying between Calcutta and Australia, was aroused from sleep by a gun shot. Snatching his steel helmet and life jacket, and calling to Cadet Simpson in the next cabin to bring him a sweater, Bellew made for the gun mounted on the after-deck. He, the cadet and one, Gunner Jones made ready to fire, though they could see nothing through the sights and could only judge the position of their attacker by gazing down the beam of the searchlight playing upon them. Presently an order was received to abandon the gun, and a moment later a boarding party of Germans arrived and gave the officers and crew of the *Nowshera* fifteen minutes to abandon ship. They were then taken in a motor launch to the raider, searched and issued with metal identity discs. At 4.30 a.m., Captain J. N. Collins, the Master of the *Nowshera*, was taken to the raider's deck to watch the end of his ship. Fourteen time-bombs had been put on board her, these exploded in rapid succession, and in a few moments the *Nowshera* was on her way to the bottom.

Her crew found themselves prisoners upon the *Narvik*, a vessel of some 9,500 tons, equipped with nine quick-firing guns, six anti-aircraft guns, a seaplane and six torpedo tubes. The *Narvik* had been operating in Australian waters, and had been engaged on laying mines in the Bass Straits. She had on board the crews of three other vessels which had suffered the same fate as the *Nowshera*. They were kept below on poor rations, but otherwise in conditions which were 'reasonable', being allowed two hours' exercise a day on deck. The *Narvik* made 'two or three rendezvous at sea with different raiders' including the *Admiral Scheer* and a large tanker, the *Dixie*, flying American colours. Eventually Bellew and the rest were transferred to a prison ship, the *Storstadt*, and in this eventually reached Bordeaux. Conditions on the *Storstadt* were very bad. Before the voyage was ended, the water allowance was reduced to one cup per day and the last fortnight of the voyage was spent under hatches.

Once on land, Bellew made up his mind to escape as soon as possible. From a French workman he procured a small map of the South of France, saved his bread ration and stowed it together with 'thirty hard biscuits' in a pillow case. The day came when he and the other prisoners were put in a train to be taken to Germany from the camp, where they had been confined since coming ashore. Bellew, with a Mr. Harper and two Australians, jumped from the train shortly before midnight, and hid in a wood. Their situation was precarious and it would have gone ill for them had they been caught for, being determined to help their country in every way they could, they had 'kept drawings of the different raiders they had met at sea with full details of armament etcetera'. Setting course by the sun and heading south and south-west, they crossed the Loire at Blois, being greeted by the German guards on the bridge with a polite 'bonjour', and presently ran into two French gendarmes. 'I tried to bluff them, telling them we were Americans and had lost our papers, but it wouldn't work, so we decided to tell them the truth. This did the trick. They even asked us for our autographs, and shook hands with us and wished us good luck.' The behaviour of the French gendarmes on the wrong side of the line dividing Occupied from Unoccupied France was by no means unique. The travellers met similar treatment at the hands of the Vichy Military Authorities who gave them travelling warrants to Marseilles where they separated. Bellew, who could speak Spanish, determined to make for Gibraltar through Spain, and one evening reached the Spanish border. Night was coming on and he spent it 'at the foot of the mountains by a stream into which I had previously fallen'. On the next day, after a troubled night during which he had been awakened by heavy rain, thunder and the roaring of a tree set on fire by a thunderbolt, he presented himself to the Spanish authorities 'at a small village near Espolla'. This was a mistake, for he was at once deprived, in the best Fascist manner, of all his possessions and money and flung into gaol in the company of three English soldiers, two Belgians, a Spanish Republican and his girl, and 'fleas, lice, cockroaches and rats in abundance'. Thence they were taken, manacled, to Figueras, where Bellew, from a balcony, witnessed the beating-up by a sergeant of some Spanish Republican prisoners. 'Three of them were knocked senseless . . . one of them had an arm missing, another was blind of both eyes.' Two days passed and Bellew and his English companions were then taken to Barcelona through the streets of which they were led 'our wrists tied together with rope'. After an unsuccessful attempt to get into touch with the British Consul, Bellew was removed again, this time via Cervera, to Zaragoza, where he made the acquaintance of his fourth Spanish prison. 'It was congested with Republican prisoners . . . so close to each other that they had difficulty in turning over from one side to the other. Most of them ought to have been in hospital . . . this night a Spanish prisoner was flogged badly for several hours; next day he died.' From Zaragoza Bellew eventually reached the notorious 'transit' camp, Miranda de Ebro. Here he remained for several weeks, being visited by the British Military Attaché who 'brought us tinned food, tea and cigarettes'. Eventually the order for his release came. He travelled to Gibraltar and thence by ship to Greenock.

Six weeks after the loss of the *Nowshera*, the *Nalgora*, a cargo vessel plying between the United Kingdom and Bombay, met her fate in the Atlantic. It was on the 2nd January and the ship was heading for the Cape and had already reached warm latitudes when she was struck by two torpedoes. The Purser, who was deaf, at first thought that a steampipe had burst in the engine-room. The pronounced list which the ship took soon shewed him this was not so and he returned to his cabin to collect the ship's papers. He had hardly entered it, when the *Nalgora* 'gave a sudden big lurch, the cabin door slammed to and I could not open it'. At that moment the Purser heard the signal, 'Abandon ship', being blown on the steam whistle, and remembered that somewhere among his kit was an old chisel. He found it, hacked the lock off the door and reached the deck just in time to slip down a lifeline into a boat. As he entered it, a shell from the submarine which, not content with torpedoing, was also shelling the *Nalgora*, struck her and set her afire. Nearby, in another boat, were Captain A. D. Davies and Cadet Cockcroft, who had been taking a bath when the ship was struck. He spent the next eight days in pyjamas and a fine new bridge coat belonging to somebody else, and suffered no ill effects.

The boats lay beside the sinking *Nalgora*, their crews keeping their heads well down, for they were occasionally swept by bursts of machine-gun fire. At dawn, Captain Davies secured his boat to two rafts and was joined by the boat in charge of the Second Officer. The Purser's boat had parted company during the night and he and its occupants were picked up two days later. Captain Davies was not so fortunate. He took his Second Officer on board 'with all his survivors, including the cat, and then set sail for the Cape Verde Islands'. Progress was at first difficult until the rudder, which had been missing all night, was discovered underneath the Indian donkeyman, who 'proudly produced it' from beneath his thwart. The voyage lasted eight days and the men were on short rations. The ship's cat fared best, for 'ordinary rations were supplemented by tiny fish which we were able to catch for him'. The monotony of the voyage was relieved by the manoeuvres of a twelve-foot shark who 'tried to grasp one of the men steering' and remained 'swimming alongside with a nasty look in his eye' till Captain Davies drove him off with a boathook. 'In more favourable circumstances,' he notes, 'it (the voyage) would have been very interesting as the water teemed with marine life.' After eight days, land was sighted and they were saved.

The men in the lifeboats of the *Nalgora* were more fortunate than those of the *Gairsoppa* (Captain G. Hyland), the next of the Company's vessels to be sent to the bottom. *Gairsoppa* was one of the 'G' vessels of the Company's Fleet. They were designed as cargo ships and their average complement was nine Europeans and sixty-four Indians. The *Gairsoppa* joined an eight-knot convoy at Freetown at the end of January 1941. Four days out, the convoy ran into bad weather and the *Gairsoppa*, having on board a large quantity of pig iron, found it increasingly difficult to keep station. Her consumption of coal rose so quickly that she had eventually to make for the nearest port in order to replenish her bunkers. On 14th February she left the convoy at dusk and two days later, about breakfast time, a large four-engined aircraft circled her and made off. The *Gairsoppa* continued her voyage but at half-past ten that evening, a torpedo, fired without warning, struck her in No. 2 hold on the starboard side causing, among other damage, the fall of the foremast which carried the main and emergency wireless aerials. No S O S could therefore be sent, and, as the vessel was settling down by the head, Captain Hyland gave orders to abandon ship. Two and perhaps three boats were launched under fire from the light automatic machine-guns of the submarine which had fired the torpedo. There was a heavy swell and the launching of the boats was accomplished with great difficulty. The boat in charge of Mr. R. H. Ayres, the Second Officer, later Assistant Cargo Superintendent, drifted aft, narrowly missing the ship's propeller now out of the water and whirling round above the heads of the crew. Once clear of this danger, she lay off, hove-to on an emergency sea anchor, and those on board her watched the *Gairsoppa* sink bow first, on fire fore and aft. She had remained afloat for twenty minutes. In the lifeboat were eight Europeans and twenty-five Indian seamen. After waiting all night in the hope of keeping in touch with the other boats (none were seen save one waterlogged with two Asiatic seamen on board who were taken off), the sail was hoisted at dawn and course was set due east under reefed mainsail. Driven by a strong westerly wind, the boat plunged ahead through a heavy swell. Much of the fresh water had been lost at the launching and only one and a half beakers remained intact—enough to give two dippers of water a day to each man on board. After the second day 'it was found impossible to swallow the biscuits (which were the main ration) due to the dryness of mouth and throat'. The Europeans occupied the stern seats, the Asiatics were for'ard and amidships where the boat cover gave them some protection from the spray. They were issued with blankets, the Europeans giving up theirs so that their Indian shipmates might the better withstand the cold. Despite this precaution, deaths occurred from frostbite from the fourth day onwards, and to this was added deaths from drinking salt water, which drove those who drank it mad before they died. Thirteen days after the torpedoing, the Lizard was sighted. By then, only three Europeans and four Asiatics were still alive. The weakened men strove to bring the boat to a beach which was descried through a narrow cleft in the cliffs. The wind, however, blowing directly on shore, was too strong, and, on drawing near, the boat broached to; all on board were flung into the water and the four Asiatics were drowned. She presently righted herself and the three Europeans climbed back again but were unable to maintain their position for long, for the boat once more capsized. One European then swam to the rocks but was washed off, apparently injured about the head; another was lost through being unable to retain a hold on the then overturned boat and the one survivor was picked out of the surf by lifeboat men who had been summoned by four London evacuee children; while gathering firewood from the cliffs they had observed the plight of the boat. Ayres, who was subsequently awarded the M.B.E., was the only survivor of this terrible voyage. The fate of those in the other boats 'has never been known'.

Three weeks later, another of the Company's ships, the s.s. *Nardana,* was sunk in the same waters. She was one in a convoy of fifty-two ships escorted by H.M.S. *Malaya* and two destroyers. At 2.50 a.m. on 8th March, the Senior Officer of the Watch reported that 'there seemed to be a bit of trouble in the middle of the first column. Lights were flickering.' The Captain (C. E. White) ordered him to keep a good look-out for a rocket, and at that instant one clove the night sky just as a dull thud, sending 'a shudder throughout the ship', shewed that a torpedo had gone home. Mr. A. H. Burfoot, one of the ship's officers, was in bed. Jumping out, he hurriedly put on jacket and trousers over his pyjamas and sought to tie the laces of his shoes. 'My fingers shook too much to knot a bow and cursing my fear I left the laces hanging loose.' Whatever were his feelings, Burfoot knew his duty. He emptied the ship's safe and picked up a case already packed with the ship's papers. Then 'I flashed my torch round the cabin. There was a fleeting picture of sheets flung back, socks hung on a chair, collar and tie on the table.' Burfoot then hurried on deck where he met the Captain. 'Outside his cabin the Old Man called me to tear up the confidential books. We ripped their backs and tore their pages, scattering the bits to the wind. "We'll have some clothes from my cabin," he said. I went inside with him. He opened the wardrobe and passed out coats and mackintoshes. A pile they seemed, as I took them to the boat.' It was lowered with difficulty into the water and Burfoot, the Third Officer, the Second Engineer and, finally, the Captain slid down the life-line and landed 'in a rush upon the close-packed bodies beneath'. They pushed off from the side and then 'a light shewed briefly in the water a short distance away and we heard a shout. We rowed towards it, but made little way. One moment the oars were deep in the water, the next they were swinging impotently in the air . . . once more we heard the voice, that of the Junior Engineer, in the water. There was little desperation about it; just "I can't keep up much longer". Then the light went out.' By this time the men in the boat could no longer see their ship, though 'here and there the small pinpricks of light flickered in the darkness. A sea anchor steadied us, but we retched our hearts up.' Dawn broke on 'the bleak grey waste of sea . . . the Old Man had decided to steer for the Cape Verde Islands 600 miles off. Nobody spoke of being picked up. We sailed like a cow.' One of the two destroyers escorting the convoy was seen on the horizon. As she approached 'we waited, too filled with private thoughts to speak . . . then fear gripped us when she turned away. With hands fumbling in their anxiety we lit a flare which sputtered and burnt with a fierce low light. Slowly it paled, then went out and left only a thick white smoke. We watched the destroyer. After long, dreadful minutes, back came an answering flash and she turned towards us once more. Soon she was close enough to use the loud-hailer and an impeccably accented voice told us to sail in up to the lee quarter.' Seven days later the survivors of the *Nardana* landed safely at Gibraltar. They mourned the loss of three European and sixteen Asiatic shipmates.

The *Nalgora*, the *Gairsoppa* and the *Nardana* were all sunk in the first quarter of 1941. By then the war had reached a new stage. The Battle of Britain had been fought and won. London and other English cities were stoically enduring a nightly onslaught from the air. Wavell had driven Graziani from the Western Desert and Cunningham had captured Eritrea and Italian Somaliland. Mussolini's gimcrack Empire was falling to pieces and his invasion of Greece, begun six months before, had utterly failed. For the moment, prospects in the Mediterranean seemed brighter, until it became known that Hitler was on the march to the rescue of his hard-pressed ally. In the last week of February, the British Government decided to send troops to Greece in a gallant, if vain, attempt to support a most brave ally. Most of Wavell's army found themselves in Thessaly, Attica and the Peloponnesus. They were supplied by ships sailing from Port Said, and among them was the s.s. *Homefield*, one of the Company's cargo vessels of some 5,000 tons. After waiting twenty-three days for mines laid by German aircraft to be swept from the Suez Canal, the *Homefield*, with thirteen other ships, made for the Piraeus. All went well until the western end of the Island of Crete was reached and the convoy had entered what had become known by them as 'Bomb Alley', the Mediterranean counterpart of that already famous in the Channel and the North Sea. Almost at once an alert was sounded, the Luftwaffe appeared, and the *Homefield* 'received a good drenching from four near misses'. Surviving this attack, she reached the Piraeus, discharged her cargo, and on the morning of 1st April put to sea once more with nine other ships, all returning empty to Egypt for further supplies. At dusk on the next day, the Third Officer, Hector Maclean, hearing anti-aircraft fire, made for the bridge where he saw 'up above us a formation of nine planes hovering like vultures, awaiting their prey'. Four minutes passed, and then, one by one, they began to peel off and dive towards the convoy. Maclean went to his battle-station beneath a mass of concrete built round the wheelhouse and from there watched the Second Officer 'manning and firing our entire armament by himself—a single Lewis gun . . . suddenly there was a shout from Captain S. Kiely (the Master) "Look out, there's one on us." A plane was screaming down on our foremast. There was a second of intense silence. Then a shower of cement and a roar which told us we had been hit.' Two bombs had burst on or in the *Homefield* and she began to list to port. She was abandoned and all the crew got away in the boats and were presently picked up by H.M.A.S. *Voyager*. She landed them at Alexandria just in time to wave farewell to another of the Company's vessels, the s.s. *Quiloa*, who was putting to sea on what proved to be her last voyage.

Like the *Homefield*, she was carrying a cargo to Greece. It consisted of 'a regiment of muleteers with their mules and stores and 500 tons of railway rails'. Unscathed by a number of attacks on the way across, she reached Salamis on 9th April where she lay for two days under frequent but unsuccessful air assault. Eventually the Master, Captain S. C. Brown, went ashore only to find the port of Piraeus in a state of chaos caused by the explosion of the *Clan Frazer*, which had been bombed and hit while discharging ammunition. 'The ship had disappeared and had blown up the rest of the docks and pieces of her were littered about the streets.' Eventually, by good seamanship, the *Quiloa* was brought to a small temporary jetty in Scaramanga Bay and the mules discharged. During the operation, four air attacks were made but once more without success. Not until Easter Monday, 14th April, were the Luftwaffe able at last to put a bomb into this staunch vessel. Then, a dive-bomber dropped a number of bombs on her, one of which holed her just above the waterline. Captain Brown decided to beach his ship and this was successfully accomplished. For the next three days the deck officers made and fitted a large cement box over the hole made by the bomb and on Saturday, the 19th, two corvettes, the *Hyacinth* and the *Salvia*, made an effort to take the *Quiloa* in tow. The *Salvia* was commanded by one of the Company's Chief Officers, J. I. Miller, D.S.O., D.S.C. and Bar, killed later on during the war. Neither his efforts, nor those of the Commander of the *Hyacinth*, were successful. Despite the jettisoning of many of the iron rails, the *Quiloa* remained immovable and still subjected to heavy bombing attacks. Eventually orders were received to abandon her and Captain Brown led his men by devious ways to Nauplion where a ship was found which took them to Suda Bay in Crete.

By then they had been joined by the survivors of another of the Company's vessels, the s.s. *Goalpara*. She had been hit in the same attack which had damaged the *Quiloa* and, like her, had been beached. The Chief Officer, G. R. Mudford, who was later to survive the sinking of the *Gogra*, had collected his crew and led them through Athens, and then forty miles on foot to the Corinth Canal. Here they had taken cover in wooded country from the frequent air attacks, and here Mudford exchanged his portable typewriter, which he was tired of carrying, for three fried eggs. Eventually they, too, found a ship and reached Crete. From this island both ships' companies were evacuated successfully to Alexandria, having taken part in one of those gallant actions which are a feature of the earlier stages of most great wars fought by this country. A handful of men, equipped with courage and resolution rather than with a sufficiency of weapons, engage vastly superior forces of the enemy, in an effort to win time. So it was in 1794, in 1914, and again in 1939 to 1941; and so it must ever be while Great Britain prepares for war only after war has broken out.

While these things were happening in Greece, farther east matters were slowly moving to a climax. Mistiming his rebellion, Raschid Ali, who had seized power in Baghdad at the beginning of May, was a fugitive at the end of the month; but his fate did not deter another and an older dictator, Reza, Shah of Persia, from continuing his support of Germany. In August it became necessary to overthrow him. Troops for this purpose, who had in the spring been brought to Basrah in several of the Company's ships, among them the *Nevasa,* crossed the Persian frontier, and others, taken in small vessels down the Shat el Arab, attacked and captured the great oil port of Abadan and the smaller port of Khoramshahr. During the mêlée, a 'B' class ship of the Company, which was proceeding down stream in pilotage, came under rifle fire—the only casualty was the cat—and, nearer the Gulf, Captain Gregory of the *Ikauna* was, to his annoyance, prevented from completing the discharge of her cargo by the assault on Bandar Shahpour. A few days later a 'B' class ship took the deposed Shah from Bushire to Bombay and exile, and at the end of the year Captain Baber of the British India Company earned praise and gratitude from the Admiralty for his share in the towing to Massawa of a great floating dock captured at Bandar Shahpour.

From the early autumn of 1941 until the end of 1943 the Company's ships plying between the Gulf, Indian and, on occasion, American ports carried very large quantities of supplies for Russia. These were unloaded at the rail and road head of Khoramshahr and sent on their long journey across Persia to the hard-pressed Russians. The part played by these ships in this much-needed aid was no inconsiderable factor in the success which attended it.

The list of those ships of the Company carrying passengers and cargo which were lost in the first twenty-seven months of the war must be completed by the s.s. *Winkfield* and the s.s. *Devon*. The first struck a mine in the Thames Estuary on 19th May 1941, and broke her back. Eight of her crew were killed by the explosion when at their posts in the engine-room. The remainder were picked up by drifters. Lalla Rukman, Seacunny, was later awarded the British Empire Medal 'for meritorious service'. He was one of the last to leave the sinking vessel. The s.s. *Devon* was lost on 19th August, when she was intercepted by the German raider *Komet* masquerading as a Japanese ship, the *Royoku Maru*, in latitude four degrees south and longitude ninety-two degrees west. The crew were taken on board the raider, which sank the *Devon* by detonating bombs in her engine-rooms and stokehold. The crew were subsequently taken to Germany where they remained prisoners for the rest of the war.

Thus, before 1941 was over, out of fifty-eight ships plying the seas on the lawful occasions of the Ministry of War Transport or, as with those who went from Egypt to Greece, under the orders of the Admiralty, ten had been lost. One, the *Gambhira,* never put to sea but served nevertheless by becoming a block-ship at Scapa. Others, such as the *Durenda,* damaged by three bombs on her way from Alexandretta to Port Said, and the *Matiana,* shaken by a near miss from a bomb when in the Liverpool docks, had had narrow escapes. Still others, like the *Howra,* the *Dalgoma,* the *Gamaria,* the *Ikauna,* and the two sisters, the *Kistna* and *Kola,* fitted as cased-petrol carriers, were beginning or carrying on careers distinguished by unremitting hard work on the part of their crews and by that unobtrusive, never-failing service which is the hall-mark of the Merchant Navy alike in peace and war. Still others, the *Orna,* the *Barala,* the *Itinda,* to name but a few chosen at random from the records, were ever on the move, with passengers and cargo about the Seven Seas. The men who manned them ran the same risk as their less favoured comrades in those ships which fell victims to the assaults of the enemy. They were more fortunate. That was the only difference between them.

Before the war ended, the Royal Navy had taken over ten of the Company's vessels, and the Royal Air Force two. It was among these that the heaviest losses in proportion to their numbers was sustained, for no less than five of them were sunk. The first to suffer this fate was the s.s. *Mashobra* (Captain P. Taylor), one of the Company's 'M' class vessels built to ply between London and Calcutta with 150 first-class passengers. The *Mashobra* went to the Fleet Air Arm as a Depot Ship, and as such remained at Scapa until May 1940 when she joined the force under the command of Admiral of the Fleet Lord Cork and Orrery engaged in operations against the port of Narvik in Northern Norway.

On 11th May she arrived in Norwegian waters and at once attracted the attention of German bombers. For a time their attacks, which took place at intervals during the next fortnight, were unsuccessful. They were delivered for the most part from high altitudes and the bombs missed their target. On 25th May, however, at ten to five in the afternoon, the enemy changed his tactics. Three Heinkels came over to deliver the usual high altitude attack, but on this occasion they were accompanied by a dive-bomber which made straight for the *Mashobra* and dropped a heavy bomb on the port side just for'ard of the bridge. The Officer of the Watch saw the bomb leave the aircraft and had time to broadcast an order for everyone on board to take cover or lie down. This prompt action undoubtedly reduced casualties and these numbered only three slightly wounded, but the damage caused was very extensive. No. 3 hold was flooded, but the vessel got under way before a second bomb fell precisely on the spot where she had been lying. She was too badly holed, however, to make a return to England possible, so she was beached and her guns and stores salvaged, and the Naval authorities destroyed her before the expedition quitted Narvik.

The *Karanja* narrowly escaped destruction by fire. In the spring of 1940 she had been converted from her peace-time passenger rig to a Trooper, and was presently to become a famous Infantry Landing Ship. Between her first and second transformation, she sailed from Bombay as Commodore Ship of a small convoy made up of the Company's vessels, *Kenya, Talamba, Rajula* and *Rohna,* all on their way to England to begin their special war service. On Monday, 10th June 1940, 'there was a cry of "Fire!"' reports one of the officers of the Royal Ulster Rifles, the battalion on board. 'We all tumbled out to grab our clothes. . . . It appeared that the seat of the fire was in the main baggage hold but little could be seen for the dense smoke.' Water, pumped into the hold, had no effect and an attempt to shift some of the cargo was defeated 'by the fierce heat and smoke'. *Karanja* altered course so as 'to obtain a cross-wind to keep the flames away from the woodwork of the cabins'. Eventually, the Master, Captain Bell, flooded the hold and thus extinguished the fire. The water was then pumped out and those sent to investigate reported not only that all the baggage had been burnt or destroyed by water but that 'the fire had been started by a primitive time bomb'. The remaining ships of the convoy were thoroughly searched but nothing of that kind was found within them, and all in due course reached Durban.

No further casualties occurred among these Naval Auxiliaries for nearly a year. By then the campaign in the Mediterranean had entered a new phase. The brief, heroic Grecian adventure was ending as the new barbarians poured through the gates of Thermopylae, and Wavell's men—what was left of them—made for the coast. Far to the south the s.s. *Juna*, re-named by the Admiralty H.M.S. *Fiona*, was plying to and fro between Alexandria and Sidi Barrani as a Convoy Service Ship. It was off this port that, on 18th April 1941, she met her fate, being bombed and sunk by enemy aircraft.

Eleven days later a similar fate befell H.M.S. *Chakla*, engaged upon a similar service. She, too, became the victim of German bombers as she lay in the harbour of Tobruk whither she had gone with supplies for the beleaguered garrison. This class of vessel was particularly unfortunate for, before the year was out, one of her two sisters, H.M.S. *Chantala*, had joined her at the bottom of the same harbour and the other, H.M.S. *Chakdina*, had been sunk in the Eastern Mediterranean on her way to the same fatal destination.

The *Gurna* was more fortunate. Early in the war she was fitted out as a mine carrier in Singapore, but since in those days there was little demand for her lethal wares in Eastern waters, she was presently sent to the Middle East. February 1941 found her stationed in the Great Bitter Lake in the Suez Canal Zone, and there for months she supplied with mines three of His Majesty's submarines, the *Roqual,* the *Cachalot* and the *Narwhal,* who were then operating in the Eastern Mediterranean. Though several times attacked by the Luftwaffe who claimed to have 'hit her squarely', the *Gurna* remained undamaged throughout this period.

Only two ships of the Company joined the Royal Air Force. One of them, the *Manela* (Captain J. A. Cleeve), was to see most varied service in places as far apart as Sullom Voe in the Shetland Islands, and the tropical harbour of Diego Suarez. During the early months of the war, she became the mother ship of two famous flying boat squadrons of Coastal Command, Nos. 201 and 240, armed with Saros and Stranraers, both obsolete and slow and, from time to time, of 210 Squadron flying the famous Short Sunderland. For some little time before the actual outbreak of war, the *Manela* had been engaged in preparing for it, and her officers and men were no strangers to the Royal Air Force. The transition from peace to war, therefore, took place with little break in normal routine, save for one moment on a cold, grey morning when a sentry's bayonet was presented at the chest of her Captain. 'Shortly afterwards,' he records, 'it was decided that the ship hardly gave enough scope for fixed bayonets.' There ensued a period of hard work and little leisure. There were 'a thousand and one things needed to keep the (flying) boats in the air. Bomb scows proved to be especially fractious and, in any inclement weather, of which there was quite a lot, used to fill up at their moorings and float with just their noses showing above the water.' Other marine craft proved scarcely less temperamental and had frequently to be hoisted on deck for attention to their propellers. Being moored and consequently swinging with the tide and the wind, 'the telegraph cable and the ship's own anchor seemed to have a marked regard for each other and . . . got themselves tied up in some most remarkable tangles' of which the unravelling consumed many hours of labour in cold and discomfort.

To hard work were soon added the attentions of the Luftwaffe and, being unarmed, R.A.F.A. *Manela* seemed to her crew to be the 'practice target for greater things to come'. In the circumstances, the presence of an anti-aircraft cruiser and a squadron of Gladiators based on Sumburgh was reassuring, and the *Manela* sustained no hurt. And through all this time the flying boats went to and fro on patrol across the North Sea and 'the grey waters' stretching to Iceland and the Pole, 'flying in all kinds of conditions and weather', to the admiration of the seamen. The monotony of the work was varied by the ingenious salvaging of a Gladiator, and by a cinema rigged in No. 4 hold. The aircraft was suspended between two of the *Manela's* boats and floated off at high tide from the beach of a small neighbouring island where it had made a forced landing; the cinema provided films and a stage for the only too rare ENSA concert party. So passed the first winter of the war. Then, in April 1940, the arrival of a 'rather old Norwegian gun-boat . . . packed with men who had escaped from German hands on the other side of the sea' gave promise of sterner things. But not, at least at first, for the *Manela*. Sailing on 23rd April for a re-fit, she found herself, once it had been carried out, attached to the Fleet Air Arm. The Board of Trade ensign was hauled down, the White hoisted, and the *Manela* prepared to sail for Narvik when news of its capture sent her instead to the Clyde. There, while lying in the Gareloch, she narrowly escaped injury or destruction when a bomb from a German aircraft burst alongside and wounded the Second Officer. June found her back with the Royal Air Force, first as a ferryboat carrying stores and equipment to the Isle of Islay—she was the largest ship ever to enter the inner anchorage of Port Helen —and then at Loch Foyle where an emergency flying-boat landing place was established. Here the *Manela's* crew, who could by then regard themselves as highly qualified technicians, gave aid to some of the fifty four-funnelled American destroyers placed so opportunely at the disposal of this country during a particularly critical stage. Though very welcome, they were far from new and had not fared 'too well in the Atlantic gales'.

From Loch Foyle the *Manela* presently set sail for Iceland, via Glasgow and Sullom Voe, where she took on board another famous squadron of Coastal Command—No. 204. Arriving in April 1941, she remained for four and a half months at Reykjavik. The most memorable of the days spent there were those when the Squadron, in whose service she was, was searching for the *Bismarck*. The report from one of them which found her was one of the factors causing her destruction.

From Iceland, that 'stark and inscrutable land of geysers and glaciers', the *Manela* went to the palms and torrid sunshine of Bathurst and Freetown on the west coast of Africa. Here let this old ship, built in 1923 but, like Johnnie Walker, still going strong, remain for the moment.

The *Dumana* also joined the Royal Air Force. Designed as a passenger and cargo carrier, she was equipped with 200 berths and, after being chartered by the Air Ministry, was fitted out as a complete Base Ship with workshops, a galley, a bake-house, a recreation room, and a troop deck for five hundred men. The saloon was divided into two Messes—one for the officers, the other for the sergeants.

The music room became the Operations Room. She spent the years 1939–40 in Port Said, Alexandria, Malta and Gibraltar. In 1941 she was closely concerned in the evacuation of our troops from Crete. 'Always by far the largest ship in the convoy,' records her Purser, S. F. W. Diesch, 'she received special attention from enemy bombers.' They did not, however, succeed in hitting her, though three times she visited Suda Bay, then dominated by the Luftwaffe. In all the air attacks the only damage caused to this ship was to the Purser's typewriter, 'which was blown off his office table with sad results to its mechanical efficiency'. After her adventures in Crete, she moved to Bathurst, Gambia, presently to become one of the main operational centres of Coastal Command. There she remained until towards the end of 1942.

The third kind of war service performed by the Company's Fleet was carried on by the vessels converted into hospital ships. Upon them, at least, fortune smiled, for despite the number and variety of their voyages and the constant peril of their new calling, all—save one, the *Talamba*—were still afloat when the war ended. Two of them—the *Vasna* and the *Vita*—had been built as mail and passenger boats for service in the Persian Gulf. The *Vasna* joined the Royal Navy in September 1939 as a hospital ship designed to act as an additional hospital at bases where medical facilities ashore were not extensive enough to meet all the demands of the Fleet. A vessel of some 4,000 tons, built in Glasgow in 1917, she carried a self-contained hospital unit of 280 beds, assembled in seven main wards, with a number of 'fresh air' wards established on the after well deck and poop. There were two operating theatres, an X-ray room, a laboratory and a dispensary. The medical staff consisted of Royal Navy doctors and surgeons, sisters belonging to Queen Alexandra's

S.S. VASNA

S.S. AMRA

Royal Naval Nursing Service and the sick berth ratings of the Royal Navy. The Master of the ship was Captain R. A. H. Bond, who, with the Purser and crew, were servants of the Company. In 1940 the *Vasna* was at Scapa Flow, serving as a base hospital for the Home Fleet, and in due course returned to Liverpool in time to suffer damage from an air raid in December. After serving six months with the South Atlantic Squadron, she rejoined the Home Fleet in July 1941. Her sister ship, the *Vita*, continued to voyage between Bombay, Karachi, Bahrein and Basrah until May 1940, when she, too, became a hospital ship. The *Amra* remained on the Calcutta–Rangoon run until the end of 1940 when she was transferred to the same duties and became a hospital ship with 400 cots. The *Karoa* underwent a similar transformation, as did the *Karapara*, which became a hospital ship in August 1940. The *Tairea* and *Talamba*, both on the Calcutta–Singapore, China and Japan service, were also transferred to the same service.

The *Vita*, after serving for nearly a year in Eastern waters, came to Port Said in March 1941, and thereafter moved between Haifa and Tobruk carrying wounded. At that time any ship who put into that port did so at her peril. On 14th April, as the *Vita* was leaving the swept channel, she was attacked by a number of enemy dive-bombers, one of whose missiles struck the pole of her main-mast and, being thus deflected, fell into the sea. Had it not done so, the ship would in all probability have been sunk. As it was, the blast caused the engine-room to fill to sea level, and presently the water began to rise in the stoke-hole and in Nos. 3 and 4 holds. The vessel then took a heavy list to port and her steering gear broke down. H.M.S. *Waterhen* took her in tow to an anchorage two miles outside the boom entrance. Then, after dark, the *Vita's* 430 patients were transferred to the warship by the light of burning candles. Throughout these difficult operations the seamanship of H.M.S. *Waterhen* was, records the Master of the *Vita*, magnificent. The crew was transferred to another of His Majesty's ships and eventually Naval tugs towed the damaged *Vita* to Alexandria, at a speed of five knots. When on passage she was again attacked by enemy aircraft but without result. Repaired at Alexandria, she became a Naval hospital ship and until the end of 1941 was based on the port of Aden.

It fell to the *Karapara* to replace her at Tobruk. The *Karapara* was one of the more elderly of the Company's vessels —she was built in 1915 for the Bombay–Durban run—and began the war as a troopship, continuing thus until August 1940 when she was fitted out at Bombay as a hospital ship. Her first campaign in her new capacity was that fought in Abyssinia and she went to and fro between Port Sudan and Bombay or Karachi with Indian wounded. On 17th April 1941, when near the Island of Perim, she was ordered to land her patients at Aden. Hardly had she done so when she was ordered to proceed to Suez with all despatch. On reaching that port she experienced her first air raid, which 'brought home to us the peculiar feeling of helplessness in a hospital ship with no means of defence and made us all think of what might happen with patients on board'. At Suez the Master, Captain J. G. Radge, was told to take his ship to Tobruk to replace the *Vita*, bombed and damaged a short time before. The Master made all preparations, the medical staff set up emergency theatres, the crew looked to the boats and to the gear for hoisting on board cot cases, and all were eager to go into action.

On the first night out, the *Karapara* passed the stricken *Vita* in tow, 'not a very encouraging sight'. The perils ahead were very great; for at that period of the war, the spring of 1941, Tobruk was a magnet for the Luftwaffe and the Regia

Aeronautica. The small harbour was choked with shipping, most of it on the bottom, and the town was under siege. The *Karapara* arrived at three o'clock one afternoon in the middle of a sandstorm. This made navigation difficult, all the more so since the Master had not been issued with a chart lest, if some mishap occurred, it should fall into the hands of the enemy. He had, however, been allowed to consult one of these aids to navigation at Port Said and to commit the details recorded upon it to memory. With such recollections of the complicated state of the harbour as he could call to mind to help him, and aided by an armed trawler which went ahead to pilot him through the boom defences, Captain Radge took his ship into a harbour 'full of wrecks, both British and Italian'. The first object to meet his gaze was the sunken *Bankura*, one of the Company's Persian Gulf vessels on which he had once served as a junior officer. Her Master and Chief Engineer were helping to load wounded from a small wooden jetty into 'boats of all descriptions including lifeboats' from the wrecks. A grimy Sea Transport officer and a still grimier Naval officer in charge, 'both very cheerful', ordered him to 'embark all patients as quickly as possible and get out'. While in harbour the orders were that the blacking out of the ship must be absolute. Any light shewing would be extinguished by rifle or gun fire. In the circumstances Captain Radge was anxious to sail before dark, but it was 10 p.m. before the *Karapara* put slowly out to sea with 549 patients on board, including seven Italians, all stretcher cases. The wind was blowing fresh from the south-south-east, and the desert sand once more drew a welcome veil over the proceeding ship. Scraping past the 'wreck of an Italian cruiser', the *Karapara* approached the boom but the trawler leading her missed the opening and signalled 'Please anchor'. The signal was made too late and before the vessel lost way she had struck the boom and was 'held fast by the port propeller'. From this grave predicament the *Karapara* was rescued by the courage and resource of Mr. Walton, the Second Officer. He stripped and swam to the buoy whose cable was the cause of the trouble. With great difficulty he rove a wire rope through the ring on the top of the buoy and when dawn broke the ship was riding free. As soon as the boom gate could be seen, the engines went full speed ahead and, three hours later, the Chaplain-in-Chief of the Australian Forces, who was on board, held a Communion Service on the deck. 'I think for us all,' says Captain Radge, 'it was also a Thanksgiving Service as it was surely an act of Providence that cleared us, and it was a touching sight to see those Australian warriors sitting or kneeling as best they could.' On the next day the *Karapara* reached Alexandria and disembarked her wounded. A week passed and once more the *Karapara* set out for Tobruk. She reached it and anchored in accordance with orders beside the unfortunate *Chakla*, of which the fate has already been described, and which was 'perfectly upright sitting on the bottom'. As before, the day passed embarking wounded and a heavy air raid developed at seven in the evening. For half an hour the ship was rocked by explosions and one bomb burst in the engine-room store and set it on fire. The flames were put out 'with hand pumps and chains of fire buckets', for the deck service and fresh-water pumps had been put out of action. The engines and the steering gear were in a similar condition. Those on shore who had time to look at the ship observed that at times it was entirely hidden by 'huge fountains of water'. Throughout the attack a large Red Cross flag hung in mute protest from the fore-truck.

By midnight Mr. Mair, the Chief Engineer, reported that the starboard engine and the steam steering gear were once more serviceable. In this crippled condition the *Karapara* put to sea helped by a tug lashed to the port quarter. 'It was an anxious time,' records the Master. 'The ship had to be steered from aft without any compass for the helmsman, as the degaussing current rendered the compass useless. The Radio Officer was at the bridge telephone and a cadet passed the steering orders to the Second Officer who stood by the helmsman. . . . At 1.15 a.m. we cleared the boom defences, cast off the tug and proceeded on our voyage to Alexandria at half speed on one engine.' None of the wounded had been hit in the air raid and the only casualties were two of the crew wounded by flying splinters and two who afterwards suffered from deafness. All ended happily with a dinner of celebration at the Summer Palace Hotel with the Captain and Chief Engineer of the *Bankura*, who had succeeded in leaving Tobruk in a schooner, and the four of them had so much to talk about that 'it was 1 a.m. before we broke up'.

As Hospital Ship H.T.35, the *Tairea* played a part in the Somaliland campaign, moving between the ports of Kismayu and Mogadishu and taking off wounded from the beachheads. They were brought to the ship by the crew who manned the lifeboats which were then towed out by the motor-boat.

The *Amra,* sister ship of the *Aska* sunk off the north coast of Ireland in September 1940, became a hospital ship with 400 cots on 28th December of that year. Throughout 1941 she was, like the *Tairea,* attached to the forces which fought the Somaliland and Abyssinian campaigns. From the ports near the fighting—Mogadishu and Massawa—she took wounded as far south as Mombasa and Durban.

The *Karoa* and *Talamba* passed the first year of the war as troopships, and it was in 1940 that they were both converted into hospital ships. The first survived all the years of fighting, the second met her end off Sicily in circumstances presently to be related.

The soldiers of one Queen and three Kings had been carried to the field of operations by the Company ever since 1857 when, it will be remembered, the 35th Regiment of Foot was brought from Ceylon to Calcutta to play a part in the quelling of the Indian Mutiny. Since that date, ninety years and more ago, the tradition of service to the Crown might with truth describe itself as 'Purveyors by Royal Warrant of His Majesty's Armed Forces'. When, therefore, in 1939, war came once more, the Company's troopships, four in number, of which two had been built especially for the purpose, were immediately available. Their ranks, if a military metaphor is permissible, were soon swelled by others of the fleet, of which twenty-seven were eventually called to the colours.

The first of these thirty-one ships to take an active part in the war were the four regular troopers—*Dunera*, *Dilwara*, *Neuralia* and *Nevasa*. Of these, two were modern, *Dilwara* and *Dunera*, built in 1936 and 1937 respectively, the two others being veterans of the ocean, having carried regiments of the British Army during the regular trooping seasons since 1912 and 1913. They had known the First World War, now they were to play a part in the Second.

The *Neuralia*, whose name was a shortened form of that born by a famous hill station in Ceylon, first saw action as far back as 1915 when as a hospital ship she visited Suvla Bay and later on Salonika. It was in those years that her connection with the fighting men of Australia began. In 1940 it was renewed when she was one of the ships in the second convoy of Australian troops which reached the Eastern Mediterranean in the late spring of 1940 shortly before Italy declared war. After they had gone ashore at Port Said to join the troops guarding the canal, the *Neuralia* sailed to Cyprus and returned with a full cargo of Cypriots anxious to leave an island threatened with conquest and occupation. Braving the dangers of the Mediterranean, she next sailed from Port Said through the Straits of Gibraltar to Dakar where she took on board two thousand French native troops and set course for the Bay of Biscay. A thousand miles out, news was received of the fall of France. Night had fallen and the ship was turned round, course being set for Freetown. When, however, next morning the French officers on board perceived the sun to be rising on the wrong side of the ship, they were not long in enquiring the reason. The news was broken to them and when at last they could be induced to believe it, like the passengers on the *Madura* far away to the North en route for Falmouth, they broke down 'with tears streaming from their eyes', but agreed to go on to Freetown. Presently the *Neuralia* was ordered to return to Dakar where she disembarked the unhappy French and then, after narrowly escaping capture and detention by the 'Pétainists' of Casablanca, put in to Gibraltar. Then ensued a period of carrying refugees, some of them to Jamaica, where a small wooden town had been prepared for them. Among these unhappy people were Gibraltarians, Cypriots, French Colonials, Foreign Legionaries, Czechoslovaks, Poles, Jews, and Americans. On returning from the last of these trips the convoy, of which the *Neuralia* was a unit, was repeatedly attacked by U-boats over a period of several days. 'Many ships were lost, but a few still remained to arrive safely.' She was among them.

Such was the first part of this old vessel's war service. Her sister ship, the *Nevasa*, began her long and honourable career as a trooper in 1914, but, like the *Neuralia*, served throughout most of that war as a hospital ship. Towards the end, she reverted to her former status and in July 1918, when carrying American troops across the Atlantic, fought a brisk duel on the surface with a German submarine and escaped unscathed. After some years as a passenger vessel, she was converted into a permanent troopship in 1925 and remained as such until 1948 when she was finally broken up. During the first two years of the Second World War, like the *Neuralia,* she carried troops from Southampton to Bombay and then other contingents from India to the European theatre. She also took safely away from Busreh May 1941 British and Indian women and children sent out of Baghdad and other Iraqi towns when Raschid Ali rebelled against his master and for a few brief weeks it seemed that Germany might fulfil her dream and become mistress of the Middle East. More will presently be related of both these gallant ships, one of whom was to perish four days before VE-Day and the other to sail 305,898 miles by the time that day dawned.

Of the two modern-built troopers, the *Dunera* was wholly engaged on transport service from the very beginning. In the period covered by this chapter she visited twenty-six different ports, calling thirteen times at Suez, nine at Aden, six at Durban, five at Port Sudan, Mombasa, Colombo, Port Said and Fremantle, four times at Gibraltar, twice at Port Lyttelton, Melbourne, Dakar, Casablanca, Bombay, and Massawa, and once at Malta, Singapore, Wellington, Liverpool, Freetown, Takoradi, Capetown, Sydney, Penang, Mogadishu and Berbera. Such voyaging shows at once the size and might of the Empire and of the steps taken to defend it. In the *Dunera* one wide staircase panel is covered with the badges of the various units she carried during the war.

The *Dilwara,* her sister ship, was, like her, especially designed as a trooper and bore a traditional name in the trooping service. The early days of the war were spent in carrying troops from South Africa to Egypt through the Red Sea. When Italy joined hands with Germany, the *Dilwara* was more than once attacked by aircraft on these voyages, but no harm befell her, no doubt because, as her surgeon observed, 'they flew at such a height that they were only just visible to the naked eye, as little silver specks'. These tactics did not prevent 'Woe Woe' Ansaldo, the lugubrious Italian military commentator, from occasionally heartening his listeners by reporting the sinking of the *Dilwara,* and on one occasion, when ferrying Italian prisoners of war, the ship's company had great difficulty in persuading them that this was, in fact, the name of the ship. Before the *Dilwara* was engaged on this traffic, she took part in the Greek campaign and carried back to Egypt Australian troops whose 'high morale' was very much in evidence. Throughout the daylight hours of this short voyage she was under air attack from dive-bombers, some of which descended to mast height. The ship's gunners and the Australians engaged the enemy hotly and the *Dilwara* was not hit. It was for services rendered in the evacuation of Greece that Captain Sampson was awarded the D.S.C.

So much for the seasoned regular troopers in this first and very critical period of the war. Hard though they worked—and their sailing schedules shew how little time was spent in port—they were unable unaided to deal with the huge volume of military traffic required by the situation. To them, therefore, were added at short intervals twenty-seven ships who, in normal times, carried passengers or cargo. Of these, the *Barpeta* is already familiar by reason of the rescue in the Persian Gulf of a crew of a Royal Air Force bomber. Soon after this incident she abandoned trade for Military Store Service and in her new role carried supplies from Bombay to Aden, Suez and Alexandria. From there, when the siege of Tobruk began, she made two trips to the beleaguered port with much-needed equipment and was lucky enough to escape the attentions of the enemy. By May 1941 she was back on the Persian Gulf run carrying stores where in peace she had carried merchandise, and then, in October 1942, she became a troopship.

Her sister ship, the *Bankura,* was less fortunate. Early in 1941 she was taken over by the Sea Transport Department and was soon engaged in running between Alexandria, the Piraeus and Tobruk, her cargo in one direction being troops, in the other Italian prisoners. When Greece was evacuated, like the *Barpeta* she was sent to Tobruk with stores. On 21st April she arrived off the port at 10 a.m. with a large quantity of ammunition and stores on board. These she unloaded to the frequent sounds of sirens, but no attack developed until the evening. Then, at 6.30 p.m., a large number of German dive-bombers appeared and made a short but resolute attack. A bomb blew a large hole in the side of the *Bankura's* No. 1 lower hold and 'the vessel quickly filled with water to 'tween-deck level'. She was run aground in shallow water and several air attacks on the following day did her further mischief. The Naval authorities on the spot ordered her to be abandoned and the Master and crew presently reached Alexandria in a small schooner captured from the Italians, where, as related, they met with Captain Radge and celebrated their deliverance.

The *Dumra* was part of that small fleet which transported General Cunningham's South African and African troops to Kismayu in Somaliland. She was the Commodore ship and carried stores of all descriptions, a large proportion of them being petrol and water. She also had on board a four-gun anti-aircraft battery and 200 stevedores. The landing was unopposed since, just before the convoy sailed, news was received that the Italians had withdrawn from Kismayu to positions north of the Juba River. Though the necessity for fighting to secure the port had vanished, that of speed remained. Within an hour of dropping anchor, supplies were being rushed ashore by lighter, for the position had been described as 'quite desperate', and this, though the ships were only twenty-four hours behind schedule.

In those days, with resources stretched to the utmost, the armies of the Empire conducted their campaigns with little margin or none. After discharging her stores, the *Dumra* sailed away but was back within a month to take on board and transport to the Middle Eastern theatre of war an anti-aircraft battery and some thirty guns taken from the Italians, together with 'sufficient ammunition to maintain them in action for a number of months'. By then Kismayu had already lost its main importance, for the speed of the advance was growing greater and greater. The *Dumra* and the *Sofala*, another of the Company's vessels, did their utmost to keep pace with the advancing armies, and made first Merka and then Mogadishu their ports of supply. Until May 1941 both ships 'plied without stopping between Mombasa and the Somali coast' and there is little doubt that if it had not been for their efforts the vigour of the campaign could not have been maintained. That may be fairly deduced from an observation of General Cunningham, who said at the time 'in other campaigns it has been a case of the dog wagging the tail, but in this one it is the tail that wags the dog'. The 'tail' was composed of these two ships, and when all was over, they received the warm congratulations of the Army on a 'splendid effort' which had done so much to bring the operations to a successful end.

For the rest of the troopers, twenty-three in number,

all but one performed their arduous voyages in conditions always difficult and often dangerous, without fatal mishap. In the dark hours of 10th October 1940, for example, the *Karagola,* sailing in convoy through the Mediterranean, received two four-inch shells from the guns of an Italian destroyer which paid dearly for her temerity. By thus opening fire she disclosed her position, was at once engaged by the convoy's escort and sent to the bottom. A splinter of one of the shells, enclosed in a modestly inscribed glass case, stood for a long time in the bar of the *Karagola* as a permanent reminder of the hazard she ran that night and the passive but essential part she played in the destruction of an enemy warship.

The exception to immunity was the s.s. *Aska.* She met her end in September 1940. Leaving Freetown a fortnight before, she called at Bathurst and, on the 7th, sailed for Liverpool with 350 French troops on board, some of whom wished to return to France and others to join General de Gaulle. The *Aska* was capable of twenty knots and was not therefore in convoy. Maintaining an average speed of between sixteen and seventeen knots, she made good progress until at 7 o'clock in the morning of Sunday, the 15th, the Officer of the Watch sighted a periscope. No attack was made, doubtless because all that day, at varying intervals, aircraft of the Royal Air Force flew overhead on patrol. With the coming of night, however, this sure protection came perforce to an end; but the *Aska* went ahead at full speed. At 2.30 a.m. another aircraft appeared as the ship was zigzagging between Rathlin Island and the Maiden's Rock. At first it was thought to be friendly, but this illusion was dispelled by two heavy calibre bombs which, passing through the engineers' quarters, exploded over the engine-room. All lights went out and almost at once flames burst from the accommodation and the boat deck. Seeing them, the enemy aircraft circled and dropped another bomb which hit the fo'c'sle and set it ablaze. 'On receipt of this last bomb,' runs the Master's report, 'I decided to abandon ship.' The boats were lowered and the survivors were picked up by trawlers and later taken to Greenock by H.M.S. *Jason*. The escape of the engineers was, as the saying goes, little short of miraculous. 'My cabin was wrecked,' records Mr. Hall, one of them, 'and I found myself half buried in debris with steam and fumes entering the cabin through a huge aperture in the engine-room bulkhead. After struggling clear, I was unable to find any means of egress until the flames suddenly roared in, and I found myself near a port-hole which fortunately was not twisted so I was able to open it and get out in time. Mr. Bissett escaped in a similar manner, and Mr. Valentine thinks he emerged through the roof. . . . The cabins were blazing. . . . My boy, John P. D. Sousa, found me in a dazed condition . . . and seeing that I had no life-belt went down below and brought one up for me. In return for what he did for me that night, I would gladly keep him here . . . if such a course could be allowed. . . .'

Conduct of this kind needs no comment. It typified the spirit which inspired every man and officer of the Company, both Europeans and Indians, during those first grim years when the Empire had been pushed 'to the extreme edge of hazard'.

4

THE STRUGGLE CONTINUES

And let me pass in a night at sea,
a night of storm and thunder,
In the loud crying of the wind through
sail and rope and spar,
Send me a ninth great peaceful
wave to drown and roll me under
To the cold tunny-fishes' home
where the drowned galleons are.

D'Avalo's Prayer—JOHN MASEFIELD

Before recounting the further adventures of the Company's ships, an enterprise of great importance must first be mentioned for it played a major part in the activities of many of them. The vessels taken over by the Admiralty for specified purposes had to be extensively altered before they could be used for war, and these alterations were in many instances carried out by the Garden Reach Workshops Limited, Calcutta (manager Mr. J. B. Henderson), and the Mazagon Dock shops, Bombay (manager Mr. A. A. Wilson), belonging to the Company. In 1939 these undertakings were passing through a phase of industrial expansion and were on the crest of a wave. Material was plentiful, there were no labour troubles, and output was steadily rising. The advent of war increased it still further.

After completing their first major task, the conversion of four large ships, the property of other owners, three into armed merchant cruisers and one into an anti-submarine patrol vessel, the Company's *Barpeta, Chakdina, Chantala* and *Juna* were converted into Naval auxiliaries. The workshops then turned their attention to those units which were to become hospital ships. Among them were the *Karapara*, the *Karoa*, the *Tairea*, the *Talamba*, the *Vasna* and the *Vita*. The *Amra* was also of this number and was completely fitted out and sent to Africa. Then came the turn of the troopships, and into this category no less than fourteen of the Company's vessels entered. The *Gurna* became a mine carrier, and nine more ships were altered for the transport of horses and mules.

To these activities, which were spread over a considerable period of time, others were added. The chief among them was the building of new craft and the repair of old, most of these being the ships damaged by act of war. Among the first were such craft as 'K' class paddle and 'W' class creek steamers, Fairmile motorboats, Fleming type boats, landing craft for amphibious warfare, minesweepers and patrol boats. In the second the repairs and re-fits ranged from the installation in 127 vessels of de-gaussing gear to the plugging of a hole eighty feet high and a hundred wide blown by a torpedo in the side of the s.s. *Asphalion*. The *Durenda*, which sustained a twenty-five foot internal fracture when bombed in the Mediterranean and limped into Port Said with seventeen feet of water in No. 1 hold, was among the 161 ships who required and received major heavy repairs.

Before the war ended, in addition to conversions, refits, the setting into position of defensive armament and a large number of other alterations or additions, repairs had been carried out 'on 4,614 occasions' by a European, Anglo-Indian and Indian supervisory staff which never exceeded seventy-four, and by an 'average daily muster of between seven and eight thousand' Indian operatives.

This was one of those solid, unspectacular achievements concerning which nothing was said at the time and but little afterwards. Yet had not the Garden Reach Workshops and the Mazagon Dock Workshops pursued their arduous labours so devotedly and with such care, the number of the Company's ships on service and their efficiency would both have been far lower than they were. The talent and capacity for hard work so prominent in times of peace were intensified in war, and many a stout ship, maimed by bomb or torpedo, received a fresh lease of strength and vigour at the hands of these indefatigable shore establishments. It is time to return to the high seas.

At the beginning of December 1941, General Auchinleck's attempt to wrest the initiative in the Western Desert from Rommel and his Afrika Korps was in full progress. An intermittent tank battle, which had been raging in the neighbourhood of Sidi Rezegh, had reduced both sides to a state of momentary exhaustion, but on the 6th Rommel drew off to re-form, and on the 8th the long-suffering garrison of Tobruk was relieved. The day before, the *Chantala*, one of the Company's smaller vessels which for twenty years had plied peacefully between Calcutta and Chittagong, entered the battered, wreck-strewn harbour and, striking a mine, sank almost immediately. The Company's Fleet had suffered a further loss. Thousands of miles away, on the other side of the world, a great country's Fleet lay burning at anchor.

Japan had struck at Pearl Harbour and the United States of America entered the war.

The immediate consequences for the Company were serious. Up till then the waters of the Far East had been comparatively safe. German submarines and a raider or two had operated there and had inflicted some loss on shipping; but the strength of the assault was elsewhere, off the west coast of Africa and in the Atlantic. Now, however, that the Japanese Navy was to enter the fight, the prospects seemed grim, and indeed proved so. The situation in European and Western waters, however, as far as the Company was concerned, improved, and during the next eleven months only three of its ships were sunk in those seas.

The first to go to the bottom was the *Garmula* in July 1942. She was a cargo vessel of some five thousand tons, and, after a short period of transporting sheep and goats from Port Sudan to Port Said, became a Military Store Vessel, and in that capacity plied between Australia and the Middle East with cargoes of vehicles and stores. In the summer of 1942 she found herself in other waters proceeding from Capetown to the United Kingdom. The weather was pleasant and the voyage swift until the *Garmula* had reached Latitude 5.27 north, Longitude 14.45 west, some 200 miles north of Freetown. Then, on the evening of 23rd July, 'a tremendous crash' told her Master, Captain R. C. Brown, what had happened. Hurrying to the bridge, he looked for'ard and 'saw water pouring out of the hatchway, hatches adrift, and knew it was going to be a matter of minutes only'. After an unsuccessful attempt to send out an S O S, the order to abandon ship was given. 'By this time the fore-deck was under water and the ship was listing heavily. . . . I watched my officers and crew as they did their utmost to get the boats away and, as I watched them, I could not but admire them for their coolness and courage. There was no shouting and no panic; it was just like an ordinary Saturday morning boat-drill, but performed under the greatest difficulties. One lifeboat was lowered and managed to get clear; the second was lowered into the water but was carried inboard again by the swell and smashed on the after-deck. The two remaining boats, being on the weather side, could not be lowered at all. The ship was sinking fast but I realized that there was nothing I could do except remain where I was. A lifebuoy was hanging in a bracket nearby so I unshipped it and dropped it overboard, thinking that it might help some poor soul. I noticed then that I was all alone on the ship; all the others had gone and everything was strangely quiet. To my surprise I had no fear whatsoever. Just before the final plunge I was swept overboard and I remember turning on my back and swimming as I have never swum before. . . . As I swam, I saw the stern of the ship rise high out of the water; there was a slight noise of escaping steam, then she slid gracefully down and disappeared.' Captain Brown succeeded in reaching a damaged and capsized boat to which he clung with half a dozen of the crew. 'Then the submarine surfaced and came slowly towards us. . . . I feared we might be machine-gunned, but her Commander was quite humane; in fact he even did his best to right the second lifeboat, but the job was beyond him and he gave it up. Then he called "Captain", but no one quite knew where I was or what had become of me, and many thought I had gone down with the ship. I kept very quiet myself, and in the end the submarine made away and submerged, leaving us all alone.' Just as the sun was sinking the Captain caught sight of a raft and he and four of the crew swam to it and climbed aboard. They remained upon it all night, sharing a packet of chocolate, their only food, and at about four in the morning, a little before dawn, a shadowy vessel was perceived and presently a searchlight shone out. 'To my distress,' the Captain's narrative continues, 'it appeared to flash in every direction but where we were. After a while the light disappeared altogether.' When day came, however, the patrol vessel, H.M.S. *Pict*, was still in the offing, and eventually her look-out saw the raft and Captain Brown and his men were rescued. The *Pict* spent some time steaming up and down among the wreckage 'picking up a man here and there, some hanging on to broken spars, others lying flat on pieces of wood the size of a door. We picked up a fireman holding on to a lifebuoy, and I was indeed pleased when I saw that it was the same one I had thrown overboard shortly before the ship went down. I recognised it from its shape.' Captain Brown and the survivors were landed at Freetown and subsequently taken to Liverpool in H.M.S. *Highland Monarch*.

Three weeks after the loss of the *Garmula* came that of the *Hatarana*. She, too, was a cargo ship and had remained on service along the coast of India until May 1942, when she set out for the United Kingdom via Capetown on what was to be her last voyage. On 18th August she was leading the convoy when, at about five in the afternoon, she received a torpedo below the water-line abreast of the port after end of No. 2 hold. She immediately went down by the head, the fore-deck plating bulged upwards. The *Hatarana* sank in a few minutes, her Captain and crew being picked up by an escorting corvette.

Some three months later it was the turn of the *Hatimura*. After a period of normal service along the coast of India, she set out for Durban and went from thence to New York which she reached safely after an exciting passage. In New York she was fitted with guns for defence and sailed with a valuable cargo for the United Kingdom. The convoy, of which she was a unit, met a U-boat pack and suffered a series of attacks over a period of three days. At the end of the third day the Master of the *Hatimura*, Captain W. F. Putt, was forced to drop out of the convoy owing to a breakdown in the engine-room. Repairs were carried out and, with a great effort, the *Hatimura* succeeded in catching up the convoy on the next evening. Those on board her were much relieved, but their rejoicing was short-lived, for twenty-four hours later a torpedo struck the *Hatimura* and 'a sheet of water shot up mast-high and fell on the bridge'. The damage caused 'was more than enough to sink the vessel'. Five of the six boats were got away and, as the fourth left the ship, a second torpedo struck her, knocking the bridge down and the Captain with it. When getting into his boat the Purser, an old man, slipped from the ladder and fell into the water where he was drowned, despite the efforts of the senior radio officer to rescue him. A Chinese steward and a saloon servant were also missing, but the rest of the crew and the Captain were picked up, some of them by a Dutch vessel which had herself been torpedoed but which was nevertheless able to make port. The crew of the *Hatimura* counted themselves to be most fortunate, for their ship had been carrying a heavy cargo of high explosives which the two torpedoes might very easily have set off. The ship did not in fact explode until she was beneath the surface; then she did so to such effect that, in the opinion of Admiralty experts, she either damaged or destroyed several of the U-boats who were chasing the convoy. She may therefore be said to have avenged her own destruction.

Such were the losses among the Company's ships during what was, in many respects, the most critical year of the war. Of the other cargo and passenger carriers who survived that year of great activity it is not possible to mention more than a few. The *Howra* continued to sail up and down between Bombay and Aden and was, on one of these voyages, almost certainly saved from injury or destruction by the prompt appearance of a Catalina which drove away an enemy submarine. During the period of the monsoon, to sail those waters, even in a stout ship, was to undertake no pleasant nor easy voyage. After five days of storm, during which the *Howra* lurched her way 'slowly forward against a driving wind and blinding rain', waves 'twenty feet high' breaking and pounding 'like thunder upon her decks', a leak was discovered in No. 1 hold bilges in the forward part of the ship. The pumps were set to work, but the water gained upon them and presently the vessel, down by the head, began to lose her buoyancy until she was partly submerged. Nevertheless, she continued to plough her way through the heavy seas 'struggling', as her Second Engineer Officer puts it, 'against the elements of mighty Nature with the force of 2,300 horse power to keep her head above water like that of a drowning man struggling for life. . . . Down below, in the bowels of the ship, men toiled, struggled and sweated to maintain a head of steam. The stokers could hardly keep their balance and fire the boilers. . . . The dust from the coal hung in space like a fog.' Conditions, far from improving, grew worse, and presently it was determined to 'drill a number of holes in the collision bulkhead near the bottom to enable the water in No. 1 hold to drain into the fore-peak tank' whence it could be pumped out. Two officers in bathing suits tackled this task and by so doing saved the ship, which eventually reached Aden thirty-five feet down at the forward end, and every man aboard her 'feeling wearily happy'. Such perils were Nature's contributions to those created by U-boats.

The *Warfield*, when in convoy outward bound from Glasgow to Suez via the Cape, had a narrow escape. She was loaded with ammunition which included twenty torpedoes, 200 tons of T.N.T. and several thousand live shells. On 25th July the ship ahead of her blew up and the force of the explosion lifted the *Warfield* almost out of the water, blew down all the black-out screens and left her shewing bright lights in every direction. Her cabins were filled with 'ginger-coloured fumes', probably the fuel oil of the blown-up ship which had been turned into vapour. The *Warfield's* Master, Captain H. Goater, who was down below, ran to the bridge to find the Third Officer at the wheel 'with his arms glowing with phosphorus steering the ship clear of the wreckage. He said that he did not feel any burning so I told him to carry on.' It was then reported that the ship was on fire in No. 5 hatch and her Commander bethought himself of the 200 tons of T.N.T., the torpedoes and the live shells. An anxious twenty minutes followed until the Chief Officer could report that the fire had been put out, largely through the efforts of the Second Officer, Mr. Ralph, who had jumped straight down through the smoke without waiting for a helmet or a lifeline, with the nozzle of a hose. In addition to the fire, the *Warfield* was damaged by pieces of the unhappy vessel which had exploded in front of her and was 'literally plastered with a coating of fine wood splinters matted together with oil and dirt'. Sixteen hundred sheets of tin plate, three of them from the crow's nest, were collected, but 'not a soul in the ship received so much as a scratch'.

The two sisters, *Kistna* and *Kola*, it will be remembered, had been fitted as cased-petrol ships. Throughout that year they visited ports as far apart as Singapore and Mogadishu, and their camouflaged hulls were seen in Famagusta, Tobruk and Alexandria. With their highly inflammable cargo they helped to supply the Eighth Army in the Western Desert.

The *Mantola* and *Mulbera*, though not specially fitted up

as troopships, continued to carry drafts between India, East Africa and the Middle East. The *Ozarda*, after successfully taking some 2,000 prisoners of war and a large number of vehicles, from Tobruk to Alexandria, returned to Indian coastal service.

Of the ships remaining to the Royal Navy—five out of the original nine had already been sunk—the *Kenya* had been re-christened the *Keren*, and was presently, with the *Karanja*, to be used by the troops who were to take part in the Madagascar and North African landings, first for training purposes and then for the operations themselves.

The two ships attached to the Royal Air Force were stationary at their posts throughout this period of the war. The *Manela*, which had arrived in Freetown in October 1941, spent much of the next six months undergoing repairs or awaiting orders. But in June 1942 she went to Mombasa where she acted as Base Ship for Nos. 209 and 259 Squadrons of Coastal Command, while they were being fitted out with Catalinas. She remained there for ten months. On the opposite side of Africa the *Dumana* was performing similar services for other squadrons of the same Command engaged in anti-U-boat patrols above the slow, vital convoys.

While some of the Company's vessels continued to take part in the operations of the Western Desert, others became concerned in an enterprise of a different and less happy nature. It is one thing to fight your enemy wherever he is to be found. To be forced by so doing to engage in combat with a misguided friend is another and far less attractive necessity. In the spring of 1942 the successes of Japan in Malaya, the Dutch East Indies and Burma had radically altered the situation in the Far East. More than ever had strong Naval forces to be maintained in those waters. With Singapore lost and Trincomalee threatened, another Naval base was essential.

It lay ready to hand at Diego Suarez on the northern tip of the Island of Madagascar. To seize it was essential if raids against our convoys in the Indian Ocean were to be forestalled and if the enemy's submarines were to be adequately combated. Madagascar was French, and those in authority there paid allegiance to the Government of Vichy under the all but open control of Germany. The only persuasion which, at this most critical period of the war, would have a decisive effect was that of force, and force was used. On 5th May 1942 units of the Navy, Army and Fleet Air Arm moved against the island and captured Diego Suarez in forty-eight hours. The remainder of that summer was employed in securing the rest of the island, which passed wholly under the control of the Allies on 6th November.

Among the hospital ships attached to the Naval units was the *Vasna* which, in September, attended the landings at Majunga and Tamatave. Her place was subsequently taken by her sister ship *Vita* who, fully recovered from the damage she had sustained in the Mediterranean, spent part of November in Diego Suarez. The *Tairea* also arrived somewhat later, having at last completed her long spell on the Somaliland coast.

In addition to the three hospital ships provided by the Company, two of its regular troopers, *Dunera* and *Dilwara*, and the *Keren* and the *Karanja*, taken over by the Royal Navy, were also concerned in the Madagascar operations. The account given by Captain F. Caffyn, O.B.E., of what happened to the *Dunera*, of which he was in command, gives a vivid picture of one of the oddest operations of the war. 'We arrived in Diego Suarez,' he says, 'in a permanent howling gale (strong south-easterly trades . . . it always blows in Diego). . . . A swarm of Army officers appeared with a few Sea Transport officers, etc. The gist of their talk was that

S.S. TAIREA

M.S. DUNERA

we were to carry a hundred officers, thirteen hundred men and about seven hundred tons of all sorts of equipment.' Everyone and everything was to be on board by 8 p.m. 'At 4 p.m. the first men arrived in a panic to fix up a meal . . . and the cargo? All sorts, shapes and sizes, motor-bikes oozing oil (oh, the clean decks), broken cases, heavy cases, pieces of iron with which to plough the decks. . . . This went on until Saturday dawn, when with troop decks full and half the deck space occupied by stores we hove up and left.' The *Dunera* became the leading ship of the convoy and all arrived safely at Kilindini but had to wait off the swept channel for pilots. Presently 'out they came, three for four of us and, as I was wanted last, they gave me a miss. Was I furious? Oh no,—not with a strong current. To add fuel to my wrath a destroyer signalled "You are near the reef". I did not reply. Words failed me. In due course a pilot arrived and in I went.' Captain Caffyn was then ordered to take on board food and water for thirty days for two thousand men. This was difficult but not impossible. When, however, he was called upon to hoist on board six Landing Craft (Assault) and two Landing Craft (Personnel), each of the first weighing more than eight tons, 'our gear would not look at it'. A confabulation ensued between, first, a Lieutenant, then a Lieutenant-Commander, then a Commander, and, finally, a Captain. 'Finally the job was fixed' and in due course Captain Caffyn found his ship, of which the cargo had been discharged and re-loaded, burdened with a large dump of ammunition and quantities of cased petrol all over the deck.

Such haphazard arrangements might satisfy the Royal Navy, but they offended Captain Caffyn who, as soon as the *Dunera* was at sea, stowed the petrol in the isolation hospital. After a few days it became apparent that the *Dunera* was to take part in an assault exercise in company with the *Dilwara*, her sister ship, and the *Empire Pride*. 'Sunday 30th August was the Great Day; all my crew were tired with long hours' work getting ready, yet all were cheerful and at their posts by 3 a.m. At 3.45 down went the Assault Craft full of troops, then, in the faint light, or half-darkness, we could see them forming up. . . .' To the disappointment of Captain Caffyn, very little could be seen of the exercise because of the smoke-screens which hid the landings. 'By noon we heard the battle was more or less over. Who won? I don't know but I believe we did. . . . In the saloon that night at dinner it was a babel of talk. . . . Valuable lessons had been learnt, and it was universally felt that sooner or later the exercise would become reality.'

This conjecture was true and presently the ships, with the *Dunera* once more in the lead, set out to sea again, bound for the beaches of Majunga, in that part of Madagascar still uncaptured. Arriving off them in the night of 9th-10th September, the *Dunera* anchored and the troops went ashore. Presently the Assault Craft returned, were hoisted on board and the *Dunera* moved to the next beach where the same manœuvres were repeated. The Assault Craft moved off again and were soon lost to sight. 'There was a period of waiting, expectation, suspense, call it what you will, as it was impossible to believe we had anchored two and a half miles off the town and nobody ashore to be aware of it. . . . Time crept on and dawn began to shew, but not a sound.' This quiet, broken only by desultory machine-gun fire, continued to prevail and at 7 a.m. a message was received to say that the Governor had surrendered. The *Dunera* re-embarked her troops and then set out for Tamatave. Here, there was to be 'no attempt at surprise'. Arrived off the town, the attacking forces made a signal demanding surrender, and an R-boat was sent with an envoy. She moved very slowly until 'splashes appeared in the water close to her from machine-gun fire. Then the R-boat turned on her tail and returned at speed (comical to us watching).' A five-minute bombardment brought the Governor to reason, and before noon that day the *Dunera* was anchored close inshore 'disembarking everything and anything as quickly as possible'. The bloodless conquest ended by a return to Diego Suarez where 'as usual there was a howling gale of wind'. The *Takliwa* also took troops to Madagascar, but somewhat later.

Such were the adventures of some of the Company's vessels during the eleven months which elapsed between the events at Pearl Harbour and the first of the great counter-blows delivered by the Allies on 7th November 1942. Of the ships not mentioned by name, a few passed some of their time in dock, but the days spent idle in harbour undergoing repairs were very rare. For the most part they were all upon the high seas discharging the various missions imposed upon them by the exigencies of war. For their officers and men the worst was over, though they did not know it. From the beginning of 1943, despite the continued efforts of Germany and Japan to sever the sea communications of the Allies, on the maintenance of which victory depended, the losses at sea began slowly to dwindle. The enemy was still strong, still full of fight. The wheel had not yet come full circle, but it was on the turn.

5

THE TIDE TURNS

I saw a ship a-sinking, a-sinking, a-sinking,
With glittering sea-water splashing on her decks. . . .
An Old Song Re-sung—JOHN MASEFIELD

Early in August 1942 Captain E. Davies joined his ship, the *Urlana*. She was lying in dock at Glasgow and the Master was gratified to see, as he stepped on board, that a number of additional guns were being added to her armament. Surprise mingled with gratification when the next items to come on board were ammunition, followed by tanks. His ship was a cargo vessel, only a year old, and was fitted with a derrick strong enough to carry thirty-ton landing-craft. Two of these were taken on board and, towards the end of October, when the preparations were at last complete, the *Urlana* sailed, one of a large convoy whose complement of men, stores and guns shewed that it formed part of what Mr. Churchill was soon to describe as 'this majestic enterprise'. The undertaking to which the *Urlana* contributed was the invasion of French North Africa by a combined American and British force with orders to occupy Casablanca, Oran and Algiers, and then to capture Tunis further to the east.

In addition to the *Urlana,* the *Keren* and *Karanja* took prominent parts in these operations. All of them survived the opening phase. The *Urlana* dropped her two landing-craft a few miles west of Algiers at midnight on 8th November, and those on board then made contact successfully with the *Keren,* once the *Kenya.* The *Urlana* herself went with the remainder of the convoy to Algiers and, four days later, was one of the ships detailed to take invading forces to the small port of Bougie. After it had been taken over—captured is too strong a word—she put in to unload, and at once, with the other ships in the small port, became the target of the Luftwaffe. The attacks were frequent and severe, five British vessels being sunk. The *Urlana,* however, escaped almost untouched and eventually returned to Glasgow. Here she was once more loaded with equipment and stores and sailed for Algiers. Her next duty was to act as Commodore Ship for a convoy of eighteen merchant vessels bound for the North African port of Bone which had been captured by parachute troops early in the campaign. Yet again the *Urlana* arrived safely, although, of the five torpedoes fired at the convoy, two missed her by only 200 feet. On this voyage, three of the escort vessels were bombed and sunk. At Bone, at last, her luck deserted her. On 9th February 1943, during one of the frequent air attacks, she was struck by a bomb and damaged, but not so severely as to put her out of action. There were no casualties, temporary repairs were carried out, and she returned to Glasgow. During these strenuous days, when the ship's company were constantly at work under the wail of sirens and the loud voices of bombs, the behaviour of the cadets on board was especially noteworthy. 'They were splendid,' reported Captain Davies, 'and never hesitated to man the guns.' Setting out once more from Glasgow, this time bound for South America, fate finally overtook this staunch vessel. She was stranded and lost off the west coast of Scotland.

Among the ships less fortunate than the *Urlana* during their stay at Bougie was another of the Company's vessels—the *Karanja*. She, it will be remembered, was taken over by the Royal Navy from the Merchant Navy in July 1941, and became an Infantry Landing Ship. That summer she moved to Loch Fyne and anchored off Inveraray, remaining there, except for a short stay off Scapa and six weeks' re-fitting in Liverpool, until March 1942, when she sailed for South Africa. During this period she took part in a series of exercises of which the purpose was to train men and crews in amphibious operations. 'The proceedings,' according to Mr. D. W. Tillett, who served with her throughout, 'were novel. No books of instruction had been written, and all hands were learning and improvising from their own operations. Landing Craft (L.C.A.) had replaced the ship's lifeboats in the davits and, in addition, two more were carried under the for'ard heavy lifting derrick and two under the after. . . . The ship would be loaded with troops at Gourock and move round to Loch Fyne. After dark on the appointed night, she would be shifted to a position off the selected beach, stopped, and the Landing Craft lowered and sent ashore with the troops. Everything was made as realistic as possible by maintaining strict black-out and complete silence. . . . The ship's personnel, and particularly the Landing Craft crews, became very efficient.' They were soon to make use in tropic waters of lessons learnt in a misty Scottish loch.

The *Karanja's* stay at Durban in April 1942 was short. With other ships she sailed on the 28th, and on 5th May arrived at Ambararata Bay to take part in the invasion of Madagascar. The operations which there took place may be said to have completed the training of the ship's company.

On their completion the *Karanja* left for home and reached the Clyde on 18th September. On 26th October she left it for the last time. A large and well-escorted convoy, one of several, of which she was a unit, was bound for North Africa. All went well; the landing carried out at Sidi Ferruch, a few miles west of Algiers, was almost unopposed. On the next day the *Karanja* entered Algiers Bay and on the day following left again as Commodore Ship of a convoy bound for Bougie, one hundred and thirty miles further east. Here the landing operations proved difficult because of the surf, but soon all the convoy was in the harbour 'and the small craft started ferrying the troops and their gear ashore, speed being essential as time was to shew.' Air raids soon developed, the first, entirely unsuccessful, being made by five Italian torpedo bombers. These were followed by JU.88s, flown by experienced and resolute pilots. 'Cloud cover was ideal for the enemy. He would approach at considerable height, select his target, dive through a hole in the clouds to release his bombs, and be away out of sight behind the clouds again before the ships could find his range. The bombing was excellent and it was very galling to see the ships being eliminated one by one in this deliberate way.' Two neighbouring ships, the *Awatea* and *Cathay*, were destroyed, the *Cathay* burning all through the night. Early on the morning of 12th November, the *Karanja's* turn came. 'She was struck by at least two, and possibly four, bombs. At the time the Captain was standing on the bridge looking for'ard, and he remarked: "By God, those were close." A nearby officer replied: "Yes, sir, they are in the engine-room."' Though the bombs were small, the ship's engines were put out of action and she was set on fire. It was evidently her fate to perish in this manner, for this time the bombs were not a primitive pattern like that which had been placed in her hold in Bombay two years before, but effective and lethal incendiaries. It proved impossible to extinguish the flames and she was abandoned with some loss of life among the engine-room ratings, one part of whom escaped through one of the shaft tunnels while the other, 'who went down the other tunnel, was not seen again'. The survivors were brought back to the Clyde in the *Strathnaver* which, also at Bougie, was not hit.

The *Keren*, the Company's *Kenya*, which had also been converted into an Infantry Landing Ship, went through the North African operations without harm.

While they were proceeding, the victorious army of Montgomery was driving westward so that Rommel and Von Arnim might be caught, as they were, between two fires. The main ports of supply for the Eighth Army were for a time Benghazi and Tripoli. The *Rohna*, with troops, and the *Ozarda*, with petrol, went to Tripoli. To Benghazi, with petrol, went the *Sofala*, arriving there four days after it fell, the first British vessel to do so. The work of her launch, manned by Third Officer George Suter and the Fifth Engineer Ian MacDonald, drew praise from the Sea Transport officer for 'the great assistance you have given' made it possible 'to give our first convoy of petrol and supplies a quick despatch, and greatly assisted us to prepare for the next'.

On her return from a voyage to Malta with supplies, in the course of which she had escaped the torpedo of a U-boat, the *Ozarda* (Captain Finlay Kerr) had been quickly fitted out in Port Said to carry this inflammable cargo, and duly arrived at Tripoli a few days after its capture. The mouth of the harbour being blocked, her cargo was discharged into landing craft as and when the weather permitted. But when the entrance to the port was cleared, the *Ozarda* sailed proudly in, the first British vessel to enter the inner harbour of Tripoli. A few days later General Montgomery himself went on board to thank the Captain and the ship's company 'for the good work they were doing in bringing supplies by sea'.

Good it undoubtedly was; it was also dangerous. On the way back to Alexandria for more petrol there was a brisk encounter with a U-boat north-west of Tobruk. One of the escorting destroyers sank her. The next voyage to Tripoli was successfully accomplished, but the *Ozarda* suffered a series of heavy air attacks when lying in port and saw two of her consorts set on fire. To the assault of bombs was added that of the new 'circling torpedo', an ominous weapon which moved 'slowly twice between the *Ozarda* and an American Liberty ship, the *Samuel Parker.* As it approached for the third time, one of the cadets on the bridge of the *Ozarda* opened fire upon it with a rifle, the Master holding it in the beam of an Aldis lamp. His aim was true and the torpedo was exploded only thirty yards from the port side.

The *Ozarda* had visited Malta successfully. The *Erinpura* met her end attempting to do so. She was Commodore Ship of a convoy of twenty-three, which included the *Karoa,* the *Egra* and the *Rohna,* with an escort of eleven destroyers and sloops, and on 1st May 1943 was sailing in a westerly direction thirty miles north of Benghazi. During the afternoon an attack was made by a single torpedo-carrying aircraft, the harbinger of several more. Supported by bombers attacking from high level, they came in with great determination and torpedoed a tanker. In the dwindling light the torpedoes appeared to an eye-witness to be parachutes, and it was thought that a bomber had been hit and the crew was baling out. Disillusion was immediate. A few moments later a bomb struck the *Erinpura.* It fell through a hatch and exploded in the hold, after which 'water seemed to come in everywhere'.

The D.E.M.S. gunners, who were at their gun, were blown off the deck, and the Master, Captain P. V. Cotter, on the bridge, was knocked down by a falling column of water. Gun-layer Albert Whittle was in charge of the twelve-pounder above the poop structure. After the explosion he and his crew manned their gun once more and maintained it in action till the end. They were last seen firing heavily as the stern of the *Erinpura* rose upwards to the sky and she plunged bow first to the bottom. She sank in four minutes and the casualties were heavy, for, since the convoy was under air attack, many of those on board had, in accordance with orders, taken cover below deck. Sixty-five were drowned, the great majority Indian seamen. The Master, P. V. Cotter, owed his life to Motiur Rahman, who dragged his Captain unconscious on to a raft.

Nine days after the *Erinpura* had joined the long list of ships which for two years had sought to supply the gallant island of Malta, the campaign in Africa came to an end. The enemy was utterly broken and had surrendered unconditionally. A short pause ensued while the Allies renewed their strength, for though the blow dealt to the Axis had been severe it was not mortal, and Mr. Churchill, standing in the ruins of the Guildhall to receive the Freedom of the City, while rejoicing at the success achieved, was constrained to prophesy that there would be 'heavy fighting in the Mediterranean and elsewhere before the leaves of autumn fall'. The next objective was Sicily and against this island the British and American forces moved on 10th July.

Several of the Company's vessels were among the invading fleet or took part in the subsequent operations. The *Takliwa* and the *Rajula* carried troops to Syracuse and Augusta. So did the *Rohna*, who was in the first convoy and who subsequently returned to Algiers and became for a short time a

Naval Depot Ship. On the morning of the assault her Master, Captain T. J. Murphy, was without his steel helmet, possibly because, having a very large head, he had been unable to find one of the appropriate size. To the distress of Sebastian, his 'boy', who had been with him for many years, he went to his action station bareheaded. Sebastian was determined to protect his Master's head and clapped a soup tureen upon it, which Murphy ever afterwards wore in action.

Head-gear seems to have suffered on board the *Rohna*. Her mascot, a goat by the name of Neville, showed a great partiality for hats and once devoured a brigadier's forage cap of which its owner, an Hussar, was very proud. He complained bitterly of his loss and pointed out that its side buttons were made of gold. Captain Murphy was unsympathetic and suggested that the Brigadier's batman should be ordered to keep Neville under close observation for the next few days as he felt certain that, sound though its digestion was, the goat's stomach might be unable to assimilate the precious metal.

The *Ozarda* was also in the invasion and followed the troopships in on the first day of the landing. As at Tripoli, she soon found herself being attacked from the air and was damaged by splinters.

In the invasion of Sicily the *Dunera* was in the forefront and Captain Caffyn has described his impressions. In March his ship had carried out a number of exercises in the Gulfs of Aqaba and Suez. Their object was not divulged, but it was obvious that an enterprise of pith and moment was soon to take place. During the hours of daylight all went well as a rule, though Captain Caffyn was concerned with the difficulties of obtaining 'bulldog clips for doubling up the boat falls to hoist the (assault landing) craft.' But at night it was another matter. 'Where the Assault Craft went I don't know, but certainly not to the intended spot, and in penny numbers they returned, the occupants looking like drowned rats.' At the end of June, having embarked the 1st Special Air Service Regiment, No. 3 Commando, the 2nd Battalion of the Royal Inniskilling Fusiliers and other troops, the *Dunera* passed through the Canal, and on 4th July Captain Caffyn, slightly bewildered by the number of charts 'covering an enormous area' which had been issued to him, was told his destination. Sailing on the 7th, the *Dunera* met with a number of large convoys all converging on Sicily and escorted by many warships and aircraft. About noon on the 9th the wind, blowing from the north-north-west, increased to Force 5 and the sea got up. 'Heavy spray was coming over the fore-deck, but knowing the changeable Mediterranean I hoped it (the wind) would drop quickly and, sure enough, about 6 p.m. it came round to north by east (which would give a good lee for my landing beach), dropped almost to a calm but left rather a confused sea. At 8.15 p.m. away in the sunset or afterglow we sighted Mount Etna, a hundred miles away . . . there was still no opposition; it seemed too good to be true.'

The convoy split up and the *Dunera* made for her appointed place, reaching it about midnight, just as 'a flock of our bombers passed close over our masts. . . . They were so close that the sky seemed black with them. . . . I call them bombers, but they might have been tugs with gliders.' That, in fact, was what they were.

By 1 a.m. the Assault Landing Craft had been lowered and got away 'in two minutes'—the rehearsals in the torrid Gulf of Aqaba had evidently borne fruit—and the invasion of Sicily had begun. 'I now had time to look round,' continues Captain Caffyn, 'and see what was happening. . . . It was a great sight—bombs exploding, flares dropping slowly down, then the A.A. defence guns busy with their snake-like tracers going up, also . . . searchlights which occasionally flashed direct on us but never stopped, so I suppose we were too far off to be seen, but it made one think. . . . As dawn came up I verified our position and there was Mount Ėtna shewing up above the smoke. Somewhere about 3.30 a.m. we saw rockets going up which indicated that our men had made a successful landing and obtained their first objective. They gave me quite a thrill as the coastline had not looked too healthy with so many searchlights and A.A. guns in action.'

Later that morning the *Dunera* moved to a prearranged anchorage, passing on the way seven gliders, of which some 'still had men standing on top being rescued. Our Assault Craft returned with fifty-two.' When at anchor the ship at last came in for some attention from the enemy, and shells began to fall near. 'The whistle of the first shell . . . was very uncomfortable. I felt surprised and hardly knew what to do. After that I lost no time in flattening out as each arrived. I had to laugh at several others flattening out on top of each other; they looked so foolish.' Altogether four shells bracketed the *Dunera*, but the fifth, which might well have hit her for the gunners had evidently got the range, never arrived. The Commandos which she had carried into action had captured and silenced the battery at that very moment.

After breakfast Captain Caffyn surveyed the scene on shore through his telescope. Among crashed gliders and purposeful men he noticed 'two glider men who looked lost as they were making west with their bikes and seemed to have no equipment . . . an injured glider man with his red beret making slow time with many rests towards George Beach. . . . Royal Engineers hunting for mines, and prisoners working at various jobs including carrying stretchers.'

As the day went by he was cheered by the sight of 'three batches of Italian troops (each of a dozen) coming down to the beach with white flags. There they sat for three hours until our troops had time to make them prisoners. . . . The main Landing Beach was just a mass of craft, large ones landing troops direct from Africa, small ones direct from ships, and also Tank-Landing Craft with their noses on the beach.' By one o'clock the *Dunera* had landed all the troops she carried and was ready to sail again. Three hours later she did so and arrived back at Suez 'where they were delighted to see us but rather surprised'.

Four of the Company's hospital ships—*Talamba, Tairea, Amra* and *Vita*—were also present. The *Talamba* was the first to reach Sicily. In the late evening of 10th July, when three miles off the east coast of that island, she was busy embarking wounded. In accordance with the Geneva Convention she was fully illuminated and her Red Cross markings were therefore clearly visible. This did not prevent a German bomber from making two vicious attacks, of which the second succeeded, a bomb striking the vessel below the water-line on the port side close to No. 4 hatch. It fell at five minutes past ten, and ten minutes later the order to 'abandon ship' was given. The boats were put into the water, but one of them, despite the efforts of the Chief Officer, Mr. H. Cameron, whose hands were badly lacerated, struck the sea so heavily that a number of Nursing Sisters were thrown into the water. One broke her leg, another was concussed and a third was heard to cry out: 'I am hanging on to a rope; what shall I do?' 'Can you swim?' asked an unknown male voice. 'Yes,' was the reply. 'Then let go the rope,' continued the male voice, 'and you'll know what to do without asking bloody silly questions.' Fortunately the casualties were small and the survivors were picked up by neighbouring craft, including the *Tairea,* who, with the *Talamba,* had served for so long in the Mediterranean. Together, the two ships had voyaged between Alexandria and Smyrna repatriating British and Italian wounded and disabled prisoners of war, and together they had visited Tripoli to aid the wounded of the Eighth Army. Now, a bomb had parted them for ever and the *Talamba* had gone to join those other hospital ships sunk by the Germans with that cynical disregard for their pledged word which would put them forever outside the pale of civilized peoples.

The *Tairea,* the *Amra* and the *Vita* presently moved on to Italy when the tide of the Allied invasion, having overwhelmed Sicily, at long last reached the shores of Europe's mainland. The *Vita* carried Americans wounded at the Salerno landings to Oran and subsequently British wounded to Algiers.

Though not a hospital ship, mention must here be made of the Company's *Nirvana.* Fitted as a 'Mule Ship', she had already carried large numbers of horses, mules and donkeys from South Africa to India. She now performed the same office in two voyages to Sicily.

The record of the activities of the Company's ships in the Mediterranean in this period of the war must be completed by an account of what happened to the *Rohna.* After her short period of service as a Naval Depot Ship in Algiers, she sailed to Casablanca and took on board a number of American harbour-clearing troops for Italy. These were transported to Naples and the *Rohna* then received orders to take American troops to India. In the company of the *Karoa* and *Egra,* she joined an east-bound convoy off Oran on 25th November. On the next day about thirty enemy bombers delivered a fierce attack, which gradually died away. It surprised Captain Murphy in his bath, and it is said that he arrived on the bridge draped in a towel with his famous soup tureen gleaming on his head. He had time to clothe himself fully before the next attack developed an hour later. It came from a single aircraft 'about six miles away on the port beam'. Keeping a careful eye upon it, Captain Murphy 'observed something behind it with flames coming out astern; it gradually overtook the aircraft but passed beneath it and turned off towards the convoy in a steep dive at terrific speed. This missile was the size of a fighter plane and when it got almost to sea level, it straightened out and came direct for the *Rohna*. It entered the ship at shelter-deck level about fifteen feet above the water-line on the port side, and exploded in a position near the after end of the engine-room and No. 6 troop-deck.' The 'missile' was one of the new glider bombs guided by wireless. Another of them had recently sunk the Italian battleship *Roma* on her way to surrender. Immediately the whole ship 'from the funnel aft was a mass of flames, the engine-room was blown to pieces' and the *Rohna* lost way. She was obviously sinking and orders were given to abandon her. The boats on the port side could not be lowered because damage to the ship's side had thrust the plates out at right-angles and they thus formed a ledge between the boats and the water. A few boats got away from the starboard side and 'were swamped by people in the water crowding into them; as there were so many troops swimming around, more loss of life was caused by their trying to crowd the boats. Everything that would float was thrown overboard.' So passed a grim three-quarters of an hour. By then 'all were away who could get away' and there remained on board, in addition to the Captain, a number of officers and three American soldiers who 'could not swim and said they would take their chance with us'. A quarter of an hour went by and then 'with a terrific noise as if the

S.S. ITRIA

S.S. ROHNA

boilers had fallen out of their chocks the good ship stood on end and went down stern first. . . . Even now I still don't know how I got away. I remember being showered with shell-cases . . . and being in the water almost immediately, hurt in many places.' Mr. J. M. Buckler, the Third Officer, towed Murphy to an upturned boat to which were clinging two of the American soldiers. 'They pulled me over the keel and held me on as I was out of action from the hips down, with my right arm useless.' Captain Murphy ends his report with a moving tribute to the 'discipline, loyalty and devotion to duty' of his officers and to the excellent conduct of the American troops, flung thus violently into the sea. Of the crew, 120 were drowned out of 195, and 1,050 troops out of 2,000. 'It was blowing half a gale and the sea was very cold.'

The Mediterranean was not the only sea to be the theatre of war. Far out in the tumbled waters of the North and South Atlantic and in the tropic seas of the Indian Ocean, a battle less spectacular but no less grim was being fought. It had begun on 3rd September 1939, and was not to end until the bells of victory rang out in London, Washington and Moscow. In 1943, though the casualties caused to the merchant ships engaged in it became gradually smaller, they were nevertheless severe. Among them were eight fine ships belonging to the Company.

The first to be sunk, the *Umaria*, was a new vessel which had left her builders, Barclay, Curle & Company of Glasgow, on Boxing Day 1941. Her span of life was a brief fifteen months. Early in January 1943, with a cargo of manganese ore, coir products, tea and rubber, she set out from Ceylon for the United Kingdom via the Cape of Good Hope. Joining a convoy at Durban, the *Umaria* reached Freetown in safety and quitted it in another convoy, a 'fast' one this time, of about forty ships who maintained an average speed of nine knots. The *Umaria* was the second ship of the starboard wing column. When passing the Canary Islands, two aircraft, presumably Spanish, flew over the convoy. A few days later it ran into heavy weather and also into an air attack. For the rest of the day—a Saturday—signals such as 'Submarines known to be shadowing convoy'—'Keep a good look-out for enemy sub astern'—'Aircraft is hostile'—kept all on board in a state of tension. At daylight on 28th March the convoy had to alter course and the *Umaria*, being on the inside, had to slow down. By then the possibility that the convoy would be attacked had been officially communicated to all ship's Captains, and detailed instructions issued for every ship to hold herself 'ready for the worst'. No attack, however, developed. But on the following night 'a smallish flash and a muffled "boomp" ' from the next ship in the line shewed that she had been hit. Parachute flares were sent up by all the convoy in the hope that a periscope would be sighted. What they revealed, however, was the stricken ship 'listing heavily and lowering her boats. . . . Eventually the murky dark descended upon us again, the rain felt very cold in the wind.'

The crew of the *Umaria*, who had been at action stations for many hours, had just dispersed when there was 'a terrific bump just as if the ship had hit a pier or dockside at speed and she at once fell, as it were, downwards forward and over to starboard, while a black column spurted up over the bridge somewhere. Next there was a black shower of water, rivet-heads and loose tea.' All went to their boat-stations and, reports the Chief Officer, 'it made me feel very proud of my Captain and crew . . . to see the splendid and orderly way in which they mustered.' The engines had stopped, but the *Umaria's* Chief Engineer reported from below that the ship was not sinking. In ten minutes she got under way once more and lurched forward, listing heavily to starboard and well down by the head. 'It needed some guts,' records the same officer, 'on the part of the engine crew on that murky night of uncertainty to go down into the bowels of the ship with a big hole open to the sea and carry on firing the boilers, knowing that, if we were hit a second time, there would be little hope of escape.' It did indeed, and it is pleasant to record that the engine-room serang Abdool Rohomon received the British Empire Medal for his leadership and example. Another of the Indian seamen, though undecorated, shewed equal courage. As look-out man, he had been on the fo'c'sle head and had seen the torpedo which, he said, 'looked just like a big fish'. Moving aft to report, he was almost over the point of impact when the torpedo struck. Though shaken by the explosion, he had remained unruffled and, making his way to the bridge, stood 'stolid, calm and good to see, an example to all of us'.

The *Umaria* wallowed on and was, reports her Master, 'steaming very well and overtaking the convoy slowly' when another explosion, caused probably by a spent torpedo from the battle still raging among the ships ahead, shook her still further. From that moment onwards her bows went deeper and deeper into the sea until the propeller was almost out of the water. The situation was now very bad and the messages from the Radio Officer, who was reporting at intervals the loss of yet more ships in the convoy she was seeking to rejoin, seemed to shew what was in store. Dawn broke over a vessel shipping sea after sea in quick succession with her fore-deck 'almost continually under water'. If speed were reduced she would not answer her helm. Gradually it was borne in upon her Captain that the *Umaria* could not be brought into port and he gave the order to abandon her. The crew took to the boats in the most orderly fashion but were reluctant to row away. 'Somehow we could not bring ourselves to leave our ship though we knew she was doomed to sink. There was no sign of any ship, only the vast rough Atlantic with the seas looking like great hills and the three boats bits of twigs.' The Chief Officer kept his boat waiting under the stern and lowered into it provisions from the ice-box which included half a cheese and a plateful of marmalade sandwiches. More provisions were lashed to rafts and the ship's cat with her two kittens brought safely down into the boat. Then 'the sun being up, we hoisted the Ensign as high as it would go. A few songs were sung . . . a last message was sent out giving our position,' and the boats pulled away. 'Most of the Indian crew donned their yellow protective suits (with hoods) so we had four boat-loads of the Ku-Klux-Klan.' All were violently seasick save one cadet in No. 4 boat who rigged the aerial for the lifeboat radio. 'Sparks got it going between his leanings over the side.' Presently H.M.S. *Wear* bore down upon the shipwrecked men who hailed her with cries of thankfulness and the information that they had plenty of food which they could take on board. 'Never mind the grub,' came a voice from the bridge, 'we want the bodies.' On board the *Wear* the crew of the *Umaria* found the crews of two other torpedoed ships. Guns began to fire, someone shouted 'They're sinking your ship.' But the Chief Officer, L. A. Bunn, was unable to watch the *Umaria* go down. He hid himself below as the *Umaria* sank at 11.04 a.m. on 30th March 1943.

Three days later the *Gogra*, as has been recounted in Chapter I, was torpedoed in the same waters.

Four days went by and then the Company suffered a third loss. The *Waroonga*, Captain C. C. Taylor, was No. 44 on the port side of a convoy of fifty ships sailing from New York to the Mersey. She was a cargo ship of some 9,000 tons and had been carrying troops and supplies between the United Kingdom and Australia. Sometimes the cargo varied, and on one occasion, early in 1942, she had been loaded with 2,500 tons of explosives which she had had to bring through the Caribbean Sea to New York. It was a voyage which stayed in the mind of her Captain, for, having braved all the known and unknown perils of the deep, he had passed through the Cape Cod Canal and Long Island Sound and had dropped anchor outside the northern entrance to New York, when the Port Captain ordered him to sea again, saying that if any mishap befell his ship in the Narrows half the city might be blown up. This order was obeyed but, having travelled with this cargo through the highly dangerous zones infested with U-boats, the Captain—and who shall blame him?—felt that the fears of the New York Harbour authorities were perhaps exaggerated. Be that as it may, he had to retrace his course and, when rounding Cape Hatteras, almost collided with a U-boat on the surface. Fortunately it was at night and the U-boat crash-dived as soon as the *Waroonga* opened fire. Her cargo was therefore safely delivered. Now, a year later, she was to be less fortunate.

The convoy sailed on in weather very cold but normal for the time of year, but on the fourth morning a U-boat pack picked it up. The convoy was beyond the reach of air cover and, the weather being very bad, the main escort had not reached it. Throughout the night of the 4th–5th April, a running battle was fought by such escort vessels as were present and the sea was soon illuminated by parachute flares. Among the ships thus brilliantly revealed was the *Waroonga* and in a few minutes she was hit by a torpedo. Soon there were seventeen feet of water in No. 4 hold, but since Nos. 5 and 6 'were full of butter and cheese', the Captain hoped that the ship would still possess enough buoyancy to remain afloat. The crew worked all night 'behaving splendidly' and gave him 'the utmost encouragement to keep the vessel going'. Dawn found her still afloat and 'given the chance of the weather improving, there seemed good prospects of making port'. But the weather did not improve, and the U-boat attacks continued. Nevertheless, all on board the *Waroonga* 'were in good spirits' though the drinking water was going bad and 'the coffee was terrible'. That evening the Commodore of the convoy was informed that the engine-room bulkhead was leaking badly but that the pumps were just able to keep the water under control and that all would still be well if only the rescue tugs which had been summoned would arrive on time. The Commodore urged the Captain of the *Waroonga* to hold on and promised that the *Tay* (escort vessel) would stand by and would not 'let me down. I liked the last bit . . . it bucked me up considerably. It was a queer feeling I had all this time; I felt that everyone on board was watching me, and I hoped that we would be able to pull through. I was on deck all the time. . . .' The weather grew worse during the night, and in the morning the ship felt 'dead' in the seaway. The after-deck was at water level and before long it was obvious that the *Waroonga* was about to settle by the stern. With the utmost reluctance, therefore, the Captain gave the order to abandon ship and the crew mustered and stood ready. The Captain remained at the traditional post, on the bridge, 'feeling rather lonely standing up there alone, but all was going as we had practised hundreds of times before, there was no panic and everyone was being quietly efficient. It was dark, cold and blowing hard.' With great difficulty the boats were got over the side and the crew was picked up by an American vessel, the *Joel R. Poinsett*, whose Master, Captain T. A. Morasson, a 'grand man', stood by and saved forty-two souls though throughout the process another attack by U-boats had developed. 'It was dangerous work and bravely done.' The Captain was picked up by a corvette, but the boat containing the Chief Officer and thirteen men was overset in the high seas and they were lost. The last sight of 'the old ship' (the *Waroonga* was launched in 1918) was of a hull 'standing nearly vertical, the funnel just disappearing'.

Before the April was out, yet another of the Company's ships—the *Nagina*—had gone to the bottom off Sierra Leone. Like the others, she was in convoy but the escort for nineteen vessels was only one corvette and three trawlers. At nine in the evening of 30th April, Captain Bird, who, with the Third Officer, was on the bridge watching the wake of the ship ahead, 'saw the track of a torpedo approaching . . . at an angle of ninety degrees about thirty feet distant on the port side.' The loud, inevitable explosion followed. In this instance so fierce was it that the *Nagina* heeled far over and the water flooded both 'tween-decks. She sank in ten minutes but only one of the crew—the Chinese carpenter—was lost, though the Second Radio Officer was struck on the head by one of the boats and killed. Captain Bird and the survivors were landed at Freetown where they were accommodated in the Seamen's Mission. The Indian crew fared worse and were given shelter in four lodging-houses. The loss of the *Nagina* led to a protest being made by the Masters of all the ships in the convoy on the failure to provide an adequate escort, even though enemy submarines had been reported active.

Thus, despite the improved prospects of the war in general, the Company had, in the brief space of thirty days, lost one ship in the Mediterranean and four in the Atlantic. But this was by no means the end. May 1943 was but five days old when the *Gharinda* met her fate. She was one of a convoy sailing from the United Kingdom to New York, and one of the escorts was H.M.S. *Tay*, the corvette which had stood by the *Waroonga* a month before. The voyage was a slow one, and for much of it hampered by a series of fierce and well sustained U-boat attacks. On 5th May, in the early evening, the *Gharinda* (Captain Rodney Stone), was hit by a torpedo on the port side near the bows and began to sink rapidly by the head though she did not list. This was fortunate for, since she remained on an even keel, it was possible to lower all the boats, but one—No. 5 which nose-dived into the sea with the ship's papers. The crew were taken off and the Master got away in the motorboat. Having gone a short distance from the ship and seeing her to be still afloat 'although the propeller and rudder were out of the water', he determined to return to her. In this he was prevented by the Commanding Officer of the *Tay*—he received an immediate award by wireless of the Distinguished Service Order for the part he played in the U-boat battle—who refused to allow this risk to be run at the height of a submarine attack and with the barometer falling. All the crew of the *Gharinda* were saved.

The *Gharinda* was sunk in the North Atlantic. A month later, far away in the south-east, the *Dumra* was torpedoed in the Indian Ocean between Madagascar and Durban. After a voyage of nearly three weeks, during which the ship's wireless had picked up 'several alarms and S O S messages', thus shewing that enemy submarines were in the neighbourhood, the *Dumra* was sailing towards Durban when, in the early hours of the morning of 5th June, in weather 'perfectly clear with scarcely a ripple on the sea' she was struck by a torpedo. The crew took to the boats which were lowered into the water, but the Master, Captain W. C. Cripps, told them to stand by as the ship might not sink. Two seconds later, however, a second torpedo struck home and the *Dumra* sank in a few seconds. Those still on board her were flung into the sea, but all save Captain Cripps and the Fifth Engineer were picked up by the boats, though several of them died later from their injuries. The submarine proved to be Japanese and, cruising among the boats, took off the Chief Engineer, Mr. H. T. Graham, as a prisoner. He was never seen again. The *Dumra's* motorboat towed the other boats towards the St. Lucia lighthouse until a heavy wave—as evening drew on, the sea got up—swamped her engine. The boats remained at sea throughout the night but, on the next morning, landed at the base of the cliffs below the lighthouse, 'the keeper having turned out from a bed of fever to guide us in'. The *Dumra* was well-known on the East African coast, especially to the Asian and African populations. Her loss was keenly felt and her memory commemorated by reproducing her picture as the centre-piece of a 'Khanga'. These are the main ornaments of African women on the coast, 'who display the latest designs in them with the same pride that is accorded to the latest dress designs in London, Paris or Inverness.'

Before the year 1943 was out, two more ships carrying cargo were lost. The first was the *Warfield*, Captain H. Goater, who, it will be remembered, narrowly escaped destruction the year before when carrying a cargo of explosives from Glasgow to Suez. She was on passage from the Clyde to Gibraltar in a convoy of some forty ships. All went well until the forenoon of Sunday, 15th August, when two four-engined enemy aircraft, flying at great height, were seen. That afternoon an attack was made by Focke Wulfe Condors which dropped several bombs without any perceptible effect. They returned to the attack about sunset and bombed the convoy for the third time. The last bomb of the last stick fell very close to the *Warfield*, lifting her out of the water, smashing the main steam pipe and blowing a hole in the ship's side. At first it seemed that she might not sink, but a closer inspection shewed that, by the manner in which the deck began to corrugate, her back was broken. The Second Engineer Officer, Mr. Deans, was killed by the bomb, but he and one Indian member of the crew—whose conduct 'was exemplary'—were the only casualties. 'When last seen in the failing light the *Warfield* was folding up in a broad "V".' The Master, the Chief Officer, J. Smail, and the Second Officer, A. Ralph, were awarded the King's Commendation for brave conduct.

The last of the Company's ships to perish in 1943 was the *Dumana*, which had taken part in the evacuation of Crete, and which had spent most of the previous year as accommodation ship for the Royal Air Force at Bathurst, Gambia. Her end came when she was on a voyage from Port Etienne to Takoradi, calling at various ports on the way to land men of the Royal Air Force. By Christmas Eve she was approaching Takoradi and all on board were eagerly looking forward to a Christmas dinner on shore. All, that is, save the troop storekeeper, who was much distressed at the loss overboard of the ship's black cat. 'I have seen it happen before,' he was heard to murmur, 'and I don't like it, I really don't like it.' His forebodings were justified. What happened next may be told in the words of Mr. S. F. W. Diesch, the Purser.

'That evening I took dinner with the Senior Purser in his cabin. Sometimes we didn't bother to dine in the saloon and about seven, our work being more or less up to date, I went into the lounge, took a comfortable chair and got stuck into that good, meaty book, Harrison Ainsworth's *Windsor Castle*. Squadron-Leader Crisp, the O.C. Troops, was the only other occupant. He was in another chair over on the port side. We hardly spoke, we were too engrossed in our books. I had my life-jacket on the deck near my chair but no torch. How I regretted its absence a little later.

'At 8.30 the bar boy came up to open the bar. I heard him put the key in the hatch latch, open up, and then the familiar tinkle of glasses. I pondered a weighty question. Christmas Eve, but I intended not to exceed two small whiskies. Should I invite the O.C. to have one now at opening time, or save my two up until later? I didn't have to ponder long. There was an almighty ear-splitting crash, the ship shuddered, the light flickered, failed and came on again. A tin fish had hit us on the port side, for'ard of the bridge in No. 2 hold. The clock said 8.33. I dropped my book (Henry VIII and Anne Boleyn no longer interested me much), picked up my life-jacket and got to my feet. Over my shoulder I exclaimed to the O.C., with an adjective: "That's our lot." As the jacket was slipping on, time stood still, there was a roar the like of which I had never heard before—it was catastrophic; it was so awful it was like an unearthly quietness. The glass roof pelted down, furniture went right and left, the lights went out. The darkness was a hot black cloud, it enveloped one, almost solid in its intensity. Instinctively I went ahead, only to measure my length over a crazy chair. Stumbling up, I groped and my hand played a falsetto note on the keyboard of the piano blown away from the bulkhead. It rasped my jangled nerves but it shewed the way out. That piano couldn't have been moved more than a few feet from the bulkhead, and on its right side was the alleyway. I found the opening and out to the top of the main companion-way, from the bridge deck. An R.A.F. sergeant came hurrying up, complete with torch. Together we made for the alleyway door out to the promenade deck. It was jammed, but luckily not too stout. Our shoulders went at it and it gave. Out in the open, on the deck, the noise was fierce. The roar of water rushing into the torn ship was like a thousand express trains tearing through a vast tunnel. One of the starboard boats was on fire. Heaven knows how it caught, as we were hit twice on the port.

'Forward to the companion, but it had been blown away. By this time the list to port was alarming. We jumped, swung, and climbed up to the boat deck over the rails. There everyone was calm and busy, but there was little or no time. The launching of the boats was terribly handicapped by the extreme list. The blocks jammed. The Third Mate, young George Reid Tate, and a couple of quartermasters tried to make their way to the deck below to free them. Nobody saw them again. I saw my senior number and said "This is bloody awful, Blondie", but he didn't hear.'

'Some of us jumped into a boat in the water, but now only eight feet or so from the deck. The man after me fell between the ship and the boat. I fished him out of the water. The Indian boat-crew and all of us were frantically trying to free ourselves from the davits, but it was no good. The *Dumana* heeled over on her side, over came the davits and we were swamped. The davits brushed my hair as they crashed and squeezed the man next to me against the boat's side. I don't know who he was, but he screamed. It was not nice.

'Then we were in the water. Down, down, I went. There were whirlpools all along the ship. I thought: "This is it. Five minutes ago I was reading, now it seems like curtains." I took deep gulps to finish it off but it wasn't decent clean salt water. I imbibed a pint or two of diesel oil. Very poor stuff for a Christmas party. Up, up, I came. My head bobbed into the open and a friendly oar was by my hand, immediately to be seized. Things looked much rosier now and the chances

Unveiling of monument at Sassandra Point erected by the local inhabitants in memory of the Officers and men who lost their lives in the M.S. DUMANA torpedoed Christmas 1943.

of survival seemed good. I can't swim more than two or three strokes, but there was plenty of flotsam about and the life-jacket was doing its stuff.

'There was general bedlam around and about. A conglomeration of noises, which together created a most unholy symphony, split the night. Not the least being the fervent ones of the saloon and deck crew calling loudly upon Allah for aid. We also were not behind in our pleas, but our appeals to our Almighty were so mixed with queer adjectives which have never graced the Book of Common Prayer, He must, if He heard, have been very puzzled to know exactly what was required of Him.

'I could now look round and riding above the confusion was the great bulk of our ship, now almost on her side and down at the head. Only perhaps fifty yards off, her grey was just skylined against the inky horizon. Slowly down she went. Up at the stern, over to port more, then more. Poised she was, about hanging. The electric siren shorted and a banshee howl of doom swept the air. Gently, gently, she slid, no fuss, like a tired old lady she parted the ocean, the sea surged over and another good ship was added to the hurricane waste of war.

'Some of us were picked up soon, others had to make the best of it all night. Just one thing after another, but one has a strong will to live. After some hours, an upturned lifeboat made a good billet for perhaps a dozen or so of us to cling to. How we clung! Dawn is always a lovely sight, and never did it have a more fervent little group of worshippers, white and brown, than that Christmas morning. Sighted by a Catalina soon after daybreak, a smoke float was dropped and the Navy hauled our party out of the water about 6.30.

'All over, bar memories; Takoradi by Boxing Night, and hospital for some. But there were over forty who were left behind sleeping with the ship who had carried them so well.'

Captain O. West, the Master, pushed off from the bridge as it became awash, having ordered all hands, as he expressed it, to 'a forced swimming parade which for some lasted all night'. A Y.M.C.A. tea canteen which remained afloat among them caused those who saw it to demand tea. Such was the spirit of these oil-smeared men, of whom many were rescued by H.M.S. *Arran*. So great an impression did the sinking of the *Dumana* make upon the inhabitants of Sassandra, close to the scene on the Ivory Coast, that they caused a monument to be carved by Georges Hamard, a local sculptor, and they set it up to remind those who pass by of the men who died that night.

Thus ended a year of triumph and disaster, but the company of every ship, from the Captain on the bridge to the Indian greaser in the engine-room, had long since learned to 'treat those two impostors just the same'.

6

VICTORY IN EUROPE

Yonder, round and ruddy, is the mellow old moon,
The red-funnelled tug has gone, and now, sonny, soon
We'll be clear of the Channel, so watch how you steer.

A Valediction—JOHN MASEFIELD

By the beginning of 1944, for the Company's ships in European and Atlantic waters, the worst was over. Only one of them was sunk before the advent of V.E. Day. Had the war continued or, more truly, had Bomber Command and the Eighth American Army Air Force failed to disrupt Germany's programme of U-boat building, this record would have been more sombre even that it is. In that year new types of under-water craft were about to be commissioned in large numbers. In shape not unlike mullet, able by means of the Schnorkel tube to remain submerged for weeks, powered by a new type of engine driven by a highly novel fuel which gave them, even when under water, speeds up to twenty knots, they would have proved a formidable foe. Many a merchant ship would have gone down before the antidote to them could have been found. As it was, the difficulties of assembling their various pre-fabricated parts and then of making them ready for sea proved insurmountable and their gutted carcases strewed Kiel harbour for months after the surrender. The Allies won the race, but only just. It was a very near thing.

By D. Day most of the Company's ships had long left European and Atlantic waters for the Far East where they had either resumed some semblance of their peace-time activities or were engaged in the war against Japan. How they fared will be described in the next chapter.

Some, however, remained west of Suez. To the *Neuralia* fell the honour of representing the Company off the Normandy beaches on D. Day. That it should have fallen to the *Neuralia* to do so was particularly appropriate, for she was one of the oldest and, with the *Nevasa,* best known of British India vessels. Having spent 1943 partly in the Far East and partly in the Mediterranean where among other duties she carried troops to Tripoli, Augusta, Taranto and Naples, she found herself at the end of April 1944 at Algiers. From this port she sailed for Glasgow and a quick re-fit and then proceeded to the Port of London where she joined other ships preparing for the invasion of Normandy. On 5th June she dropped down the river, and dawn on the 6th found her opposite *Omaha* and *Utah* beaches. This was her battle station and she went back and forth between it and Southampton until October when she returned to London for a major overhaul. In this period she made fourteen trips and carried a total of 27,055 men of the Imperial and the United States Armies.

On D. Day and the days which followed, nothing of great note occurred though the ship's defensive armament was sometimes in action against such units of the Luftwaffe as ventured over so heavily defended an area. Two 'Rocket

Pillar Boxes' (projectors, rocket) comprised part of the armament and these were heartily disliked by the Petty Officer in command of the D.E.M.S. ratings serving them and the Bofors. One day, he averred, there would be an accident; one of those ratings, the second object of his aversion, would be killed and he would have the task of 'shovelling his remains out of the Pillar Box'. That day dawned at last, or so it seemed. All the guns were in action and the projector had swung to starboard in the direction of the gun's crew. It fired, and at that moment the steel helmet of the rating whom the Petty Officer so much disliked fell off. 'There,' exclaimed the Petty Officer, instantly deciding in the face of sudden tragedy to let bygones be bygones. 'What did I tell you? It's blown poor Dick's ruddy head off.' 'And I must say,' adds an eye-witness, 'that through the smoke it certainly did look as though this is what had happened.'

While the *Neuralia* was lying off the coast of Normandy, the *Dunera* was making ready for her third invasion. She, it will be recalled, had brought Commando troops to the beaches of Madagascar in 1942 and of Sicily in 1943. Now in 1944 she was to repeat a performance by then familiar, off the coast of Southern France. The invasion took place on 15th August at 8 a.m., and the *Dunera* was chosen to carry the Headquarters Staff of the Seventh United States Army and some fifteen hundred American troops with whom all on board 'maintained the happiest relations'. She cruised to and fro in the neighbourhood of Cap Camarat until about tea-time, when she came to anchor in Pampelonne Bay. The operation was carried out with very few casualties and the Army Staff had time enough to consume stewed steak and onions or cold roast veal followed by jam tart for lunch and to dine off roast pork with sage stuffing and a chocolate Bavarois.

By then the era of sea warfare was almost over in Europe and ships which had played their parts in it, some of them for more than five years, could be released for service elsewhere. The *Manela*, which had served the flying-boats of Coastal Command so long and so faithfully on the east coast of Africa, sailed for Port Said at the end of 1944, and in January 1945 was occupied with the distasteful duty of carrying Greek prisoners of war, members of the E.L.A.S. party from Greece to Egypt. While lying off the Piraeus her crew were witnesses of the heavy fighting which went on in the streets of that port and continued on occasion down to the very edge of the sea. Having performed this task, she took a battalion of Indian troops to the little frequented island of Symi in the Dodecanese. Then in February 1945 the Air Ministry directed that she should return to the work for which she had been taken over and proceed to the Far East to take part in the invasion of Burma and Malaya. Before sailing away for good from the Middle East, she received a signal from R.A.F. Headquarters thanking the ship's company for 'good work performed'.

The *Neuralia* was also occupied in carrying Greek prisoners. Fresh from her re-fit in London, she sailed via the Azores to Alexandria and thence made three voyages with captive supporters of E.L.A.S. on board and also took Greek Government troops from Athens to various ports in Greece.

Then came her last mission. She was ordered to take some 1,700 Jugoslav refugees who had been living in camps in the Canal Zone back to their native country, free at last from German occupation. She set out for the port of Spoleto, since called Split, on the Adriatic coast. Reaching it on the last week of April, she landed her passengers and put to sea again for Taranto, there to take on board a full complement of German prisoners of war. She never reached it.

'We were coming round the heel of Italy, just turning into the Gulf of Taranto,' reports Mr. Baker, the Troop Officer on board, 'when at about 0200 I was startled out of a sound sleep by the ship shaking violently with a loud explosion. . . . At first while collecting my somewhat scattered wits I thought we were still in port and that someone had dropped a depth charge closer than he should. As this was common practice in certain Mediterranean ports at that time, the idea being to discourage saboteurs from swimming out and attaching limpet mines to ships, we were quite accustomed to bumps in the night, and I was almost prepared to turn over and go to sleep again when the alarm bells started ringing and persuaded me that it was time to get up.'

'The lights failed a few seconds after they were switched on, so it seemed that something was very wrong somewhere. Therefore I hurriedly got into some clothes and went out on deck, to find everyone else doing the same, though rather disgruntled at being disturbed. It appeared that the engine-room was already flooded which explained why the lights had failed, and in view of the ship's age—she was thirty-three years old at the time—it seemed unlikely that she could survive for very long, and the order was given to abandon.

'An interesting point with regard to the engines was told me afterwards by the Third Engineer who was on watch at the time. Being prevented by the almost immediate flooding of the engine-room from stopping the engines down there, he had had to go up to the boat deck and stop them by means of the emergency gear up there, and he said that as he did so he heard the port engine give a characteristic squeak which apparently it always did just as it stopped, so that the engine must actually still have been going completely submerged. One can only assume that having been going for thirty-three years it had got into the habit.'

The boats were cleared and lowered, and as they rowed away the crew could hear the alarm bells on board the sinking *Neuralia* ring out once more, 'probably due to the water causing a short circuit somewhere. It sounded rather eerie, that familiar sound from a by now dark and empty ship. . . . She remained in sight for some time, though we gradually drifted farther away and she was occasionally hidden from sight by showers of rain. At length we could see her no more and we could not tell whether she was still afloat or not. Other boats could be seen from time to time, as although it was very cloudy, with occasional rain, there was a bit of a moon.'

'. . . At length about 0530 dawn began to come in, and as the light got stronger we saw the ship again, still afloat and about two or three miles away. As far as could be seen she was in much the same state as she had been when we left her, therefore it was decided to sail back alongside, and if that impression was then found to be correct, to board once more. Accordingly the mast was stepped and soon, with the aid of the breeze which had freshened since daylight, we were making good speed in her direction, and I for one was feeling more cheerful. . . . We had not gone very far, though, before it could be seen that she was beginning to take a list to port, and as we watched this rapidly increased until she was almost on her beam ends. She then started to sink by the stern, and as the after end of the ship disappeared from view the forepart reared up out of the water almost vertically and seemed to hang like that practically motionless for a few moments before it, too, gradually slipped back out of sight amongst a froth of air bubbles.'

Thus sank the *Neuralia* a week before Germany's unconditional surrender. For more than thirty years she had been sailing the Seven Seas as a trooper, and had served through two World Wars. Unlike some of her younger consorts, her end had been slow, almost peaceful; but alike in life and in death she was in every way worthy to typify the spirit of the men who sailed in her and of the Company to whose Fleet she had belonged for so many years and which she had so greatly adorned.

A few days after the *Neuralia* sailed to her grave in the Southern Adriatic, another of the Company's ships, the *Gurna,* who had served through a great part of the war as a mine depot ship, put into Portsmouth. She had been extensively re-fitted in Bombay and was now 'a very effective mine-issuing and maintenance unit'. On board were a full complement of 1,650 mines. A Dutch mine-layer came alongside to take aboard her quota and had begun to do so when orders were suddenly shouted to 'hold everything'. The next day the voice of Winston Churchill was heard proclaiming victory over Germany. Rejoicing, the ship's company unloaded their deadly cargo at the Naval Armament Depot, sailed for the Port of London, and hoisted 'the Red Duster once more'.

With this happy gesture and with the passing of the good ship *Neuralia* let the tale of what happened in the Western Seas be ended. There remain to be recorded the adventures of those ships whose service was, for the most part, in waters threatened, and for a time dominated, by Japan.

7

DEFEAT IN THE EAST

We're bound for blue water, where
the great winds blow,
It's time to get the tacks aboard,
time for us to go.

A Valediction—John Masefield

That the entry of Japan into the war would hasten victory by causing the United States of America to join with Britain in the fight may very well have been in the minds of those directing the operations of the British India Steam Navigation Company; but by the time the news of the attack on Pearl Harbour reached them, it could have given them but little consolation. A situation, already dangerous and complex, was now made more so, for the greater part of the Company's vessels were in the very waters where the Japanese Navy, surface ships, aircraft and submarines, might be expected to be most active. They were, and from December 1941 until the re-conquest of Burma late in 1944 proved a constant threat and took their toll of ships.

Into the reasons why this country shewed itself so unprepared for war in the Far East it is not necessary to enter;

but this lack of preparation very soon began to affect the movement of British India ships. Within a matter of weeks Singapore, up till then regarded, and used, in military parlance, as a firm base, was first threatened, then besieged. Doubts concerning its security, aroused by the sinking of the *Prince of Wales* and the *Repulse,* grew from a vague suspicion to a horrid certainty as Percival's men reeled back through the steaming jungle and Sir Shenton Thomas urged the tin and rubber merchants to stand firm to the last. Before long the unpleasant word 'evacuation' began to be whispered over gin pahits at the Raffles Hotel and the bar of the Singapore Club and spoken aloud in the thronged, uneasy streets.

The Company's ship *Erinpura,* whose regular run was Madras to Singapore or to Rangoon with mail, was the first to leave, sailing away on 19th December 1941 for Colombo. The next was the *Ethiopia* who left on 10th January 1942, followed five days later by the *Talamba* taken over as a hospital ship in 1940. She had on board many survivors of the *Prince of Wales* and the *Repulse,* whom she landed at Colombo on 24th January. On the 27th there departed the *Rohna.* Her passengers were women and children, most of them Indians, and she left at a moment when the Island was under continuous air attacks.

The *Madura,* who had taken so many British refugees from Bordeaux in June 1940, was on 7th December 1941 on her way to Colombo. The spirits of her crew, depressed a few days later by the news that the *Prince of Wales* and the *Repulse* had gone down, were still further lowered by orders to sail on Boxing Day for Java. Confidence returned at Batavia where 'the war seemed very remote'. 'Even the Dutch seemed to be confident in all they had been told about Singapore's defences in the past,' reports Mr. J. F. Broadstreet, then serving on the *Madura.* 'This complacency was met with everywhere we went at this time, even in Singapore itself when we arrived there on about 15th January, with the Japanese only a hundred miles off in the North and still advancing rapidly. The danger of such an attitude was seen in the panic which followed on its heels when the illusions of security began to fade like morning mist.'

'I think we felt how hopeless the situation really was,' he continues, 'after our first air raid. Throughout the time we were in Singapore there were, on an average, four or five raids a day, though it was hard to judge the number as the warning system, especially towards the end of our stay, was rather erratic. But the Japanese bombing technique never varied except in the number of planes used. . . . They would come over the Island at a height of between 10,000 and 20,000 feet, quite contemptuous (they could well afford to be) of the "Brewster Buffalo" fighting planes (like ungainly little wasps compared with the awe-inspiring waves of bombers) and of the anti-aircraft barrage which, however formidable and comforting in its uproar, had no hope of stopping the bombers. Once over the Island, the Japanese would dip slightly towards their objective, and, over the target, every plane in the pack would rain down its bombs at once. The usual type of bomb employed for ordinary attacks on the city and docks was the "anti-personnel" or "daisy-cutter", a small shrapnel bomb which would explode on contact with the ground and send its blast horizontally. In a target area on which hundreds of these were concentrated, those who escaped unscathed would be lucky indeed.'

'Throughout the time the *Madura* was in Singapore, ships were arriving almost daily packed with troops, mostly Australians and Indians, to reinforce the dwindling and heroic British forces who had borne the brunt of the battle down the length of the peninsula. One day, 30th January, a troop convoy had come in, an understandable air of dejection about its passengers, and made fast not far from where we were lying. This was the biggest convoy we had seen to arrive, and we felt sure the apparently omniscient Japanese would know of it. . . .'

'It was a day of dense, low clouds, hot and steamy. In the middle of the morning the alert sirens were sounded and the guns were manned. We stood by for some time without hearing or seeing anything, and were beginning to conclude that we were out on a false alarm, when the sudden rushing of bombs sent us flat on our bellies. It was all over in a matter of seconds, but it seemed an age of volcanic upheaval. Many of the shrapnel bombs had fortunately fallen into the water harmlessly, but on our port side the cargo sheds were already well alight. A tug which had been tied up ahead of us had disappeared completely—probably a bomb had gone clean into the funnel. The *Madura* herself had been hit with one or more bombs over the after midship accommodation; one of the concrete machine-gun nests was wrecked, and the deck below was sagging perilously and on fire. Through the turmoil and the mist of cordite fumes and smoke we saw the B.I. Company's s.s. *Takliwa* steaming past us on her way out to sea. She gave us an encouraging "V" salute on her whistle as she went. The *Madura* must have been rather an alarming sight to them at that moment, and no doubt they felt not a little relief at being quit of Singapore. . . .'

'The damage to the ship proved to be not extensive, the small fire was soon extinguished, and altogether we found we had got off very lightly. An example of the unpredictable effects of bombs was found in the experience of Mr. Tomlinson, an Engineer Officer, who was asleep in his cabin when a direct hit was made on the deck right overhead; the cabin caved in and the whole deckhead landed across the bunk, but propped up in such a way that Mr. Tomlinson suffered no more than a somewhat violent awakening and subsequent annoyance at not being able to find his slippers. The sheds containing the *Madura's* cargo and, indeed, a considerable part of the dock area, were in flames, and burnt for a long time despite the magnificent work of the Singapore Fire Services. . . .'

'The *Madura*, empty and battered, was sent out into Keppel Harbour to await cargo for India. We waited three days, by which time the Allied troops had retreated back on to Singapore and, quitting the mainland, had blown up the causeway. Captain Beatty was quick to realise that our promised cargo was in all probability lost in the chaos which now reigned ashore. He accordingly made representations to the Naval authorities, with the result that, on the evening of 2nd February, we went alongside once more, took on board about two hundred passengers (about two-thirds Chinese and the rest Europeans) for passage to Java, and sailed the next morning.'

'When we left, the *Bulan* and *Mata Hari* (Malay words for "day" and "night") were still in Singapore, little ships which had been regularly plying between Singapore and Straits ports before the war, and were now under the control of the Royal Navy. They were round at the other side of the Island from us, in the much-bombarded Naval Dockyard, and stayed till the surrender, when the *Bulan* managed to get away; but the *Mata Hari* was headed off and captured by the Japanese. . . .'

'Though an outwardly calm and peaceful day, we steamed in constant expectation of attack. Plenty of wreckage was seen and several distress messages were received by the

Radio Officers during the day. . . . Yet we went through the day unmolested, and were beginning to have more faith in our luck than was good for us when, at about six o'clock in the evening, in the Dempu Strait, five bombing planes were seen approaching from the west, where the sun was already low towards the sea.'

'The guns were manned and in a minute or so we could see the yellow discs marking the planes' wings. They came in at a fair height, about 5,000 feet, far beyond the reach of our 12-pounder anti-aircraft shells, the fuses for which had been set at only about half that range by the D.E.M.S. authorities who supplied them. Accordingly we held our fire and waited for the attack. The first bombs were misses near the poop, four great splashes which drenched the gun's team and incensed them to action. As the bombers turned back for another run-in from the sun, we opened rapid fire and kept it up for the rest of the encounter. . . . They came no lower and, having failed with another four bombs to hit us, turned and came a third time from the west. This time they scored a direct hit on the after-part of the bridge deck accommodation, just below where the previous bomb had landed in Singapore. But this time it was a heavy bomb. . .'

'. . . .The scene of the impact was grim; the bomb had pierced two decks and exploded in the storeroom, completely destroying, on its way, the Surgeon's cabin and dispensary with the medical stores, but luckily just failing to penetrate into the engine-room. Five of the ship's company were dead, or died almost at once, among them Dr. Gorrie and George Lack, the Second Steward. Thirteen were badly injured. . . . None of the passengers was injured and they all behaved magnificently throughout. We were now especially grateful to have them with us, particularly the women who, with the surgeon killed and practically no medical supplies for such a task, immediately set about administering First Aid to the wounded, working through the night until they had done all they could for the sufferers. The ship's officers and crew were meanwhile fighting fires which had broken out in various parts of the wrecked accommodation, and in saving what food could be extracted from the storeroom and freezer. The fires were not very extensive, and were all under control by eight o'clock.'

'Next morning the bodies of the dead were committed to the deep, and in the afternoon the ship put in at Palembang, in Sumatra, to land the wounded. The following morning, 5th February, we proceeded on voyage to Java, where our passengers left us. . . .'

'On 12th February, on our way to Calcutta, we heard of Singapore's surrender. The acrid smell of cordite was still in our nostrils, the twisted and jagged metal and burnt-out cabins still around us so that we could not forget what we had passed through, nor what greater sufferings than ours others must be suffering. But we could be thankful, with due reverence, that the *Madura* was still a lucky ship.'

After Singapore, Rangoon. The sorry procession of incompetence and disaster moved on, and Indian troops, ill-supplied and supported only by a Chinese army in even worse case, retreated sullenly up the long length of Burma. On 4th March the Japanese forced the passage of the Sittang, and preparations were hastily made to evacuate the capital.

For many years the Company had maintained a small fleet of river launches for the carriage of mail, passengers and cargo. Four operated in Calcutta and the same number in Bombay. Those in Burma were with one exception based on Rangoon, which was also the seat of the main offices providing employment for a considerable European, Indian and Burmese staff. By the middle of February it became obvious that the city would have to be abandoned to the invaders, and Captain A. Reddish, the Company's Marine Superintendent on the spot, drew up a plan to govern the departure of the launches to places of safety further north or on the east coast. A rendezvous at Yandoon was arranged for all except the *Ailsa* which, it was considered, 'being more or less seaworthy' could go by sea to Akyab via Bassein, a total distance of about 500 miles. The launch *Hunka* was to tow the 'passenger flat', an unwieldy craft, if that is the proper term, capable of carrying 200 persons. They were to bring three days' rations but were in no circumstances to 'be allowed to carry furniture', and the number of 'perambulators and bicycles' taken was to be strictly limited. Forty tons of fuel for the *Hunka* were also be be shipped, this quantity being judged sufficient for a journey as far as Prome, a distance of 263 miles up the Irrawaddy. Following the *Hunka*, with her strange tow, would be the *Kayan*, which was to make her way to Yandoon there to await the arrival of the key men of the staff who would try to reach that place by the inland river route and then proceed to Akyab. The launches for their conveyance would be the *Maymyo* with accommodation for thirty, and the *Salona* which could carry twenty.

Such was the project drawn up with care and skill, which, if it could be carried out, would offer a reasonable chance of escape both to the launches and their occupants. The final touches were being put to it when Reddish and the others in charge were surprised by an abrupt order 'posted up at noon on Friday, 20th February' for the evacuation of Rangoon within forty-eight hours. Since, in fact, the city was not finally evacuated until 7th March, these instructions seem to have been premature; but it may be that the authorities wished to send away as many civilians as they could earlier rather than later. Be that as it may, there was a hasty change of plan and a large number of the staff were taken away by the *Warialda* belonging to the Company, and by the s.s. *Szechuen*, both of which were fortunately in port at the time. Under the command of Captain Maskell, the launches *Hunka* and *Kayan*, towing the passenger flat with a diminished complement on board, left in the midst of an air raid, sailed up the Irrawaddy and duly reached Yandoon. Thence they went on almost at once to Henzada where they were eventually joined by Reddish, Cruickshank and the other key men who had escaped in the *Maymyo* and *Salona*. Their departure from Rangoon had been far from easy. The Burmese crews of the launches, terrified by the air raids, 'had to be handled very tactfully in order to keep them from deserting', and they were not especially heartened by the sight of 'many Europeans . . . sending away their effects' and obviously 'preparing for a quick getaway. . . . In order to dispel this impression' Reddish made no effort to send away any of his possessions and in consequence lost them all.

When he and his companions arrived at Yandoon, the reason why the launches which had preceded them had left for Henzada was only too clear. The civil administration of the town 'had completely broken down', looting was widespread, and the Burmese began 'gathering round us in increasing numbers and displaying a threatening attitude'. That night the 'five remaining policemen . . . killed six Burmese' and then informed Reddish 'that they were about to give up trying to maintain law and order'.

It was amidst such scenes that the small company set out for Henzada where they joined the *Hunka* and the *Kayan*. Here the *Hunka* and the *Maymyo* were abandoned because their draught could not be reduced, and 'before we were out of sight the looters had boarded' them. At Henzada 'a break for the sea' proved impossible and the party went on to Prome and there found 'that a cholera epidemic had broken out on both sides of the river and . . . that the Indians who had walked from Rangoon were dying on the road by the thousand'. No one left the launches and a local doctor was engaged 'to inoculate all hands'. On 5th March they reached Pakokku at the junction of the Chindwin and the Irrawaddy, but here, too, there was small comfort and much confusion and cholera. They did not pause and two days later arrived at Mandalay where the state of affairs was the same as elsewhere or worse, for the 'town had been bombed . . . and was more or less paralysed'. It proved 'very difficult to get in touch with any Government official' but the Director of Inland Water Transport did his best to help and eventually the launches, which were now of no further use, were moored in the Government dockyard. After an unsuccessful attempt to journey to India together as one body, the crews were paid off, presented with the rest of the stores, enough to keep them for three weeks, and placed in the Evacuation Camp.

Reddish with Marshall and Cruickshank, having 'appeared before a committee of prominent European citizens . . . who were of opinion that we would be of little use to the military authorities in Burma', were allowed to depart to Maymyo, where they obtained exit permits and with the aid of the Chinese National Air Corporation, reached Calcutta on 1st April by air from Lashio.

In the opposite direction, away to the south of Rangoon, Captain R. Burch was in charge of the Company's launch *Yengyua*, which in normal times 'plied between Tavoy town and the sea anchorage to connect with the (Company's) steamers *Juna* and *Sir Harvey Adamson* on their voyages between Mergui and Rangoon'. Tavoy is forty miles from Siam and twenty-five by river from the anchorage. The opening days of January were enlivened by rumours of Japanese parachute troops, bombs and a brisk air fight in which an enemy bomber was shot down. Burch protected his launch as best he could with steel plates and sandbags, and 'laid in a large stock of wooden plugs . . . to stop bullet holes in the shell-plating'. When at the sea anchorage the *Yengyua* was hidden behind Grindstone Island where 'the birds sang, the water peacefully lapped the sides of my craft, monkeys scrambled on the nearby beach—the war did seem very far away. And I do notice my crew appear less anxious when we are tucked away in here out of sight of that now ominous range of Eastern hills.'

This false calm did not long endure. On 10th January the first Japanese patrols crossed the border from Siam and five days later Burch was recording in his diary: 'Our strong position is surrounded and cut off. The Japs are now between that hill and Tavoy. Over half our garrison are now lost upon that memorable hill which looks down upon Kaumedaung. . . . Hand-carts and bullock wagons stand outside the houses (of Tavoy) and whilst the poor Indian loads them up with his few belongings, the Burmans stand around in groups to jeer. . . . Went down to the launch with Johnson, Engineer Officer in charge . . . to make sure she was all ready for immediate departure. At the club in the evening, rumour says "Enemy preparing for the final push to take the town".' Two days passed and in the morning of the second Burch 'listened in to the B.B.C. on Johnson's radio whilst from his window we saw the last reinforcements marching up the road to engage the enemy. Heavy marching boots and heavy packs to fight the unseen enemy in the jungle!'

A conference was held at midnight in an upper room at headquarters between the District Commissioner, the Colonel commanding the meagre garrison, and Burch. 'At a window which faced me stood a young captain . . . gazing down into the road and looking very tense with listening. Outside an almost uncanny silence . . . and black dark.' It was decided that as the *Yengyua* represented 'the sea communications' of the Army, she should be used to bring reinforcements vitally needed from Mergui, 125 miles or so to the south. Tavoy was to be held at all costs and this the Colonel 'intended to do, though the enemy then were only about three miles away. So without more ado I agreed to stay and await orders.' Captain Burch then left and went to the air-strip for a second conference, this time with the R.A.F. commander and the District Commissioners, one of whom decided to stay with him as he had a 'very responsible and hazardous job to do. . . . With a goodbye to each of these friends of mine and fellow Tavoyans, I passed outside and slid into the front of our trusty car again, alongside my driver, old Beetlestone. We drove like the wind.' Once back at the river, Burch, to forestall a possible attempt to cut him off, took the *Yengyua* down stream to the sea anchorage. He had on board seventy-seven refugees, five of them Europeans, and before leaving had paid off the Company's local staff of whom none would take passage with him. On the way down stream, 'fearing a possible armed boarding party' from Japanese reported to be cruising about 'in large sampans', Burch flung overboard the contents of the office safe, including 'three and a half lakhs of rupees' and at dawn had safely anchored his ship behind Grindstone Island in her specially chosen hiding-place. Later that day he was ordered to Mergui and duly put to sea. He had never been to that port, 'had no means of ascertaining my position . . . no charts, only a Burma road map. . . . By mid-afternoon we were surrounded by islands.' Anchoring for the night close to one of them, he felt reasonably secure for there were no signs of war. The radio receiver broke down just as the announcer informed the listening company that 'Tavoy is in enemy hands'.

Burch slept little that night, being much occupied with 'thinking out my next scheme of action'. To press on to Mergui to bring back reinforcements to a place which had now fallen would serve no useful purpose, and on the following morning, 20th January, therefore, the *Yengyua*, whose stocks of coal and water were running low, was turned round and headed for Rangoon. She reached it two days later and Burch reported to Reddish. From then onward the *Yengyua* was employed taking wireless staff from Diamond Island and then went up the coast to Akyab. Thence she sailed to Chittagong and so in due course to Calcutta, tying up at the Outram Ghat on the evening of 23rd March, eight days before Reddish and his two companions arrived from Lashio.

In addition to the *Yengyua*, which, be it remembered, was a river boat of some 250 tons, a number of ocean-going ships of the Company took refugees from Rangoon. Among them was the *Warialda*, already mentioned, the *Neuralia*, who carried away a part of the Company's stores, the *Ellenga*, who made three trips, on the last leaving only twenty-four hours before the end, and the *Baroda*. The *Baroda* first arrived on Christmas Day, 1941, shortly after the devastating air raid which destroyed so much of the city and killed so many of its inhabitants. The city was under a pall of smoke, public services were at a standstill, and the exodus for India, which was to cause many thousand deaths, had begun. 'Men, women and children came swarming out to the ship,' reports Mr. J. S. King, the Chief Engineer, 'in sampans. . . . We had to take them aboard. No cargo could be discharged; not even coal or water could be obtained. They kept arriving all the time we were there. . . . We sailed on 27th December with some 1,400 passengers which we thought was a large number in a ship designed to carry about 800.' The passengers left at Akyab and Chittagong and by 11th January the *Baroda* was back at Rangoon where she remained until the 19th. During that time 'life was one long stand-by. Jap raids were more than a daily occurrence and all ships in the port gave warning by long blasts on their whistles.' Among the passengers who came on board was a man 'perfectly dressed . . . very tired' and speaking 'with an American accent'. He had, it appeared, been 'listening to his radio somewhere in Northern Siam' and thus received the news that Japan had struck. Gathering together all the Europeans in the place to the number of about forty, he led them through the Shan States to Burma, feeding them as best he could on the way, until they all reached Rangoon and the safety of the *Baroda*. As he came to the end of his tale his face darkened. 'I've just remembered,' he said, 'I left that radio on.'

From 19th January to the end of the month, the *Baroda* carried between 1,800 and 2,400 passengers on each voyage between Akyab and Chittagong. She returned to Rangoon for her last visit on 3rd February and stayed till the 19th off a city in which by then 'lunatics, lepers and criminals' were roaming the streets, having been released from their places of confinement. When she sailed, there were more than 3,000 souls on board: Indian, Burmese and Chinese who had come alongside, scrambled up the ship's side, and allowed the sampans which had brought them out to drift away. 'Drinking-water became a problem as well as sanitation' during the three-day journey to Chittagong. One passenger died of cholera, and doctors who joined the ship at Akyab inoculated all on board. Seven more runs were made to Akyab or Kyuak Pyu and then a final voyage from Akyab to Calcutta with 4,554 adults and about 1,500 children. The *Baroda* arrived there on 1st April and 'within an hour every passenger had been given a drink of tea, some biscuits, and a ticket to his destination in India'. Between 20,000 and 25,000 people were carried away from Burma to safety by this one ship. Her gross tonnage was 3,205.

While the Company's vessels were thus engaged at Rangoon and Akyab, another, the ill-fated *Chilka* (Captain W. Bird), a passenger ship which had been converted into a trooper, was on the way to Padang in Sumatra to fulfil a similar mission. She never arrived, for on 11th March 1942, in latitude 00.23 degrees north, longitude 95.41 degrees east, she met with 'an ocean-going submarine painted grey'. She 'appeared', reports Captain Walter Bird, who was that day so to bear himself that he was presently appointed to the Order of the British Empire, 'right aft, slightly on the port quarter, at a distance of 2,000 yards, and opened fire with two guns. I opened fire almost simultaneously and fire was sustained; with the enemy's third shot they hit one ammunition locker and the explosion caused both lockers to explode. One seaman gunner, H. Stone, had both his arms shot off and an abdominal wound.' K. M. Feast, the Second, and G. B. Hodges, the Third Officer, and a number of the crew were hit, and 'Cadet Shahabuddin sustained injuries to his hands and face and to the muscles of the back near the spine'. Nevertheless he tried to put out the fire now raging 'with his bare hands and had to be forcibly removed to safety'. He was awarded the British Empire Medal and Lloyd's War Medal.

'The gun was knocked out of action,' continues Captain Bird. 'The submarine appeared to be trying to broaden the target by steaming across the quarter, but as he altered so did I alter to keep him aft. He was firing the whole time and damage was being done to the ship's structure; nine boats were wiped out and a deal of the topside accommodation. This continued for about fifteen minutes. We then appeared to get out of range and I thought there was a chance of getting away as I was steaming at about thirteen and a half knots.

'In about a further ten minutes the submarine was again within range. He must have been travelling at at least nineteen knots and he resumed fire until . . . I realized it was no use carrying on any longer, as that would have meant the loss of the entire ship's crew, and no means of getting away. I hoisted the signal "I am about to abandon ship" and after the signal was understood, they ceased firing and allowed the crew to proceed to and get into the boats and leave the ship's side.'

'My books were dumped overside immediately the action started. I saw all the ship's boats away from the ship's side before I left her. The wounded, comprising the Second and Third Officers, a Cadet and a coal trimmer, Munir Ahmed, came away in my boat where they were attended by the ship's doctor. The wounded seaman gunner, H. Stone, got away in No. 10 boat with the Third Engineer, Mr. McAulay, in charge. Five hours later he died.'

'Five boats in all got away. After I had cleared the ship's port side in the Fleming boat No. 2, I observed on the starboard side, some distance away, a raft with two people on it. My boat was capable of carrying twenty-eight people and I had twenty-seven in it. When I turned the boat's head to pick up these people, the submarine fired one shot across my bow, and when I turned the boat's bow away again, they fired no more. I then observed the Japanese flag flying on the submarine. . . .'

'I then set a course for the nearest islands, the Mentawei. Land was sighted at daybreak on 16th March and we made towards it. The coal trimmer, Munir Ahmed, died on that day.' Captain Bird landed on Nias Island, having seen nothing of the four other boats during the passage.

'On land,' he reports, 'I was met by a crowd of natives on the beach and I tried to make them understand that it was necessary to get my wounded to hospital immediately, and I had great difficulty in getting them to understand. After an hour or so we rowed up a creek for about eight miles, as I thought to a hospital, but I found it to be a native rest house.' Bird and his men passed some hours of troubled sleep in the boat and at one in the morning started out on foot through jungle and swamp, carrying the wounded. After some hours they reached the Mission Hospital at Batak Nias Zending, where the wounded were cared for. Here Bird met with the occupants of the two other boats, and on 21st March, with the remaining members of his crew who, in two more, had landed on another island near at hand. One of them, the seacunny of No. 5 boat, reported that, 'on being called alongside the submarine after the ship had been shelled, he was asked by the O.C. submarine the ship's name and enquired where the Master was, and he reported I had gone down with the ship. The submarine crew gave them water and fresh biscuits and also gave the course to steer for land. The seacunny reported they were kind to him.'

After some days it became obvious that the Japanese were approaching. The stouthearted Captain Bird did not intend to become a prisoner if he could avoid it, and obtaining a steel lifeboat from the District Officer, set sail in it on 31st March, hoping to reach Ceylon. He had with him, in addition to the *Chilka's* surgeon and a seaman gunner, 'some of the engineers (who) were desirous of making an attempt to get away'. Having encountered adverse winds and calms, the small party had been thirty-five days at sea, when on 4th May they were picked up thirty-five miles east of Madras by a Greek vessel and landed at Karachi.

One more evacuation must be recorded before the melancholy tale is ended. Two days after the fall of Rangoon, the *Neuralia* (Captain A. A. Kay), then lying at Madras, received orders to proceed immediately to Port Blair in the Andaman Islands and take off all who wished to leave. Putting ashore a suspected case of smallpox—in normal times this would have necessitated a period of quarantine for the ship—she set out across the Bay of Bengal escorted most of the way by a cruiser. Sailing unharmed through the Manners Strait, which had been mined, the *Neuralia* passed the reefs outside the entrance to Port Blair and succeeded in entering the inner harbour, a feat never performed before or since by a vessel of her size. Taking on board all who were to be carried off, except the High Commissioner, who subsequently escaped to India in a launch with two or three of his staff, she sailed again a few hours later at two o'clock in the morning, being guided through the reefs by a launch burning a small light in her stern. On arrival at Madras the Captain of the *Neuralia* was relieved to learn that the suspected case of smallpox was one of chicken-pox.

The beginning of the Japanese war had brought disaster after disaster. Before three months had passed, great ports and bases, of which the most important were Hongkong, Singapore, Penang, Batavia and Rangoon, were in the hands of a ruthless and vigorous enemy. Trained in German methods which their native savagery had improved, the Japanese were to shew themselves ruthless alike on sea and land. Many ships fell victims to their onslaught. Among them were twelve belonging to the Company. Their fate must now be considered.

8

PERSEVERANCE AND VICTORY

The long night watch is over, and the long sea-roving done,
And yonder light is the Start Point light, and yonder
comes the sun.

Christmas 1903—JOHN MASEFIELD

On 9th April 1942, the *Vita*, fresh from the yards at Bombay where the damage she had sustained at Tobruk had been repaired, was bound from Trincomalee, her new base in Ceylon, to Addu Atoll in the Maldive Islands, there to embark a number of Naval casualties. Off Batticaloa Light she met with H.M.S. *Hermes*, an aircraft carrier, and H.M.A.S. *Vampire*, a destroyer. At that moment the vanguard of a large force of Japanese bombers appeared overhead. Ignoring the hospital ship, they made straight for the warships. The *Hermes* was 'very soon enveloped in a heavy cloud of smoke and was obviously badly on fire . . . shortly afterwards she sank and the smoke began to clear away'.

The Master of the *Vita*, Captain R. D. C. Sinclair, immediately steamed to the scene of action, lowered lifeboats and the motor-boat, and began to pick up the survivors who were 'scattered over an area of about three or four square miles. Very few of them had any means of support beyond their Naval type lifebelts.' It presently became necessary to order the motor-boat with a lifeboat in tow, to go to the rescue of the crew of the *Vampire*, bombed and sunk almost at the same time as the *Hermes*. Captain Sinclair could not take the *Vita* on this errand 'because so many of the *Hermes'* survivors were still in the water alongside the ship and round my propellers. They were swimming to our gangways.' That evening the *Vita* put into Colombo with 590 men picked up from the two ships. Of these, some 150 were seriously hurt, and the majority undoubtedly owed their lives to the fortunate chance that a hospital ship was in the neighbourhood, fully equipped to give them expert and immediate medical treatment. Among the uninjured was one of the Company's officers who on the outbreak of war had joined the Royal Navy and was at that time serving in the *Hermes*. 'I was never more pleased,' he wrote to Leadenhall Street, 'to see a B.I. ship in my life.'

In true Naval fashion the Admiral commanding in Ceylon warmly commended Captain Sinclair for saving so many lives, and at the same time reproved him for arriving late at Colombo.

After the evacuations from Malaya and Burma were over, a few weeks passed without incident. Units of the B.I. continued to carry troops to destinations as far apart as Addu Atoll and Mombasa and to sail the Indian Ocean and the Bay of Bengal, with goods and passengers on board. Their logs, dry, official records of thousands of miles travelled through long days and nights, are filled with the names of familiar ports—Bombay and Durban, Karachi and Aden, Basrah and Bandar Abbas, and further afield Fremantle and Adelaide, Colombo and Madras. Concerning many, like the *Masula*, the *Binfield*, the *Dalgoma*, the *Gamaria* and two score or so more, there is nothing of moment to report. They sailed the seas safely because good fortune and their own vigilance combined to make them so, and in their unobtrusive way helped the cause of the Allies with every gleaming mile that passed beneath their counters.

On 6th April three more of the Company's ships were lost. The *Gandara* went down off Masulipatam, the *Malda* and the *Indora* in the Bay of Bengal. These two were members of a small convoy of six of which the *Malda*, commanded by Captain H. M. Edmondson, was the Commodore Ship. On a rumour that the Japanese Navy intended to attack Calcutta, they had hastily been sent to sea together with the other shipping in the port. The *Malda*, which had just been fitted out as a troopship, was on her way to Colombo to take troops on board, the *Indora* to Mauritius with a general cargo. About 7 a.m. a small float-plane such as is carried by a cruiser closed the convoy, and flying very low crossed the bows of the *Malda*. The Japanese markings on its wings were clearly visible, and Cadet Thompson opened fire without effect. The aircraft replied with its machine-guns and then made off. Soon afterwards, reports Mr. D. J. Bardsley, 'smoke was observed right astern which owing to the speed of their approach we were soon able to identify as coming from three men-of-war, two cruisers and a destroyer'. They lost no time in setting about the destruction of the convoy which in accordance with previous instructions was beginning to scatter. The *Autolycus* of the Blue Funnel Line was the first to be sunk; then came the turn of the *Malda*. Mr. W. H. Walters, her Chief Steward, paints a grim picture of the next few minutes. The first shells demolished the saloon pantry and galley and set the ship on fire. Mr. W. Pearce, the Chief Engineer, A. Sherry, the Second Steward, and several others began the task of freeing the boats in order to lower them,

S.S. MULBERA

S.S. VARELA

for Captain Edmondson, realizing how hopeless was the situation, had given orders for the *Malda* to be abandoned.

'The shelling continued,' goes on Mr. Walters, 'and above the din of the bursting shells, splintering woodwork and rending steel, the whine of near misses was frighteningly plain. Holes suddenly appeared in the decks and bulkheads while splinters flew around with an angry buzzing sound. Flames were eating greedily into the furnishings of the public rooms and smoke was pouring out from every door and window. It is almost impossible to describe one's feelings at a time like that but the impression that I had in my mind was one of incredulous surprise and anger.'

'While I was busily engaged in freeing No. 4 boat, Mr. R. Anderson, Second Engineer, who had come along unnoticed by me, said, "It's no use, Bill", and on looking up to see who had spoken I saw him standing there, with his arms and hands, terribly burnt, held out in front of him in an attitude of appeal. I said, "It won't be long now", and very shortly after the boat swung free. At the time I thought he was referring to his poor hands, but when the boat had swung out properly, I saw a big hole in it and the Second said, "I told you it was no good", meaning the boat of course. It seems that a shell had passed through it while I was freeing it. As the Second and I moved to free No. 6 boat, several things happened at once.

'The deck piano collapsed with an unearthly moan, which caused me to comment, "There goes the Lost Chord". The Second Steward, with a smile on his face, came up to shake me by the hand and to tell me that he was so pleased that he had found that he could "take it". This helped me no end, for I was feeling pretty low-spirited by then. A gaping hole appeared in the deck through which steam rushed with an awful roar, adding considerably to the din. Four of the

Indian saloon crew appeared helping two wounded men along, so I directed them to the only remaining good lifeboat on the port side.'

'As the Second Engineer and I followed, Mr. Marshall, Third Engineer, "Paddy", Fourth Engineer, and Mr. Sale, Junior Engineer, came running along the deck towards us. Just then another salvo burst on the deck which practically cut off Paddy's left leg and Mr. Sale's feet. All rushed to their aid and Mr. Sale was carried forward, but Paddy, sensing he had received a mortal wound, told us to leave him. This we did, after giving him a cigarette and making him as comfortable as possible on a garden seat, for it was plain that he would not last very long. Surrounded by smoke and fire, he cheered and waved us on, a gallant gentleman to the end.'

Walters got down into a boat and then 'there was a terrific crash and I found myself in the water together with the rest of the fellows. . . . As I came to the surface, No. 4 boat fell on me. Luckily I still had my tin hat on, for this saved me from serious injury. I was forced beneath the surface and found myself being turned round and round along the ship's side. . . . I struggled free, came to the surface and swam clear. The ship still had way on her and as she passed I saw the Second Steward, hanging by the neck, entangled in the falls of No. 2 boat. Others were climbing the rails to try and reach him as he struggled to free himself. Suddenly he and the others who were striving to reach him fell into the water, where he was able to get free of his entanglements.

'By this time the ship was in a bad way and burning fiercely, with most of the lifeboats gone or smashed. Men were jumping from her into the sea, there to float helplessly while they watched their ship meet her doom. As she listed to starboard, before taking the final plunge, I turned my back to her for I could not bear to watch her death agony any longer. As every seaman knows, a feeling of sadness comes over one . . . when watching the end of a ship, especially if one had been in her, as I had, for some fourteen years. . . . I shall always remember her, sailing gaily along, swaying like a graceful lady, to the song of the turbines. . . .'

'. . . After a while I saw a cruiser slowly steaming away with the smoke from her guns rising upwards in the still morning air while her crew stood at stations with folded arms. While watching her steam away from the scene of destruction I found that I was quite close to a waterlogged lifeboat. I swam to it, boarded, and started to bail the water out with my tin hat. When I had sufficient freeboard, I stood on the thwarts and blew my whistle, for I could see several fellows floating in the sea round about.' Several, including the Chief Engineer, clambered into the boat. Though these and others from the remaining ships were some time in the water, no one was attacked by sharks, perhaps because, as the Chief Officer opined, the explosions had frightened them away.

'By now,' Walters goes on, 'another boat had appeared containing the Chief Radio Officer, a terribly burnt member of the Indian saloon crew and a few others. The saloon "boy" was an awful sight and his cries were heartrending, but there was little we could do for him at the time. . . .'

'We then set about the job of sorting ourselves out and arranging the watches at the oars, which were to be each of a half hour's duration. A place was made for the Second Engineer so that he could sit with his hands in the water and a splint made for the broken leg of a Marine, a floorboard being used for this purpose. I feel that I must pay tribute to the fortitude of both Mr. Anderson and the Marine, for with all the agony these men must have undergone, right up to the time they reached hospital, never a word of complaint or even a groan did they make. . . .'

'. . . During the afternoon a breeze sprang up so we decided to ship the mast and hoist sail. Unfortunately the thwart was missing but the Third Officer and myself managed to rig up a "Heath Robinson" affair which enabled us to get along quite nicely. Early in the evening breakers were sighted, and after some manoeuvring the boat was safely beached. It was found that we had landed on a sandy beach which stretched for miles either way and, as far as the eye could see, uninhabited jungle was between us and civilization.'

'Presently some 200 survivors from the various ships had collected on the shore, and they were cheered by the appearance of a Hurricane which, flying low above them, rocked his wings and then made off for help. Fires were lit and chocolates which had been presented to us by "Firpo's" of Calcutta were made into cocoa by the Second Steward.' At 7 a.m. the next morning a police inspector and a guide appeared. The wounded were placed on improvised stretchers made from 'the branches of trees and strong creepers from the jungle', and the whole party moved off through swamps and undergrowth until, weary and exhausted, they reached 'a small cluster of huts fronted by the golden sandy beach of a wide river'.

Here they met with their Captain, Edmondson, and the Chief Officer Bardsley, who had made a landfall further along the coast. A doctor arrived with morphia for the wounded and the stretcher cases were taken upstream in native dug-outs, to a point where buses would take them on to hospital. The remainder set out again on foot once more through swamps to the road-head. A second night was spent encamped in the open, and Walters, tired though he was and in pain from several injuries, 'was impressed by the beauty and eeriness of the scene—the stars twinkling through a canopy of black velvet and the hum of insects, the cries of the hyenas, the quiet moans of the wounded and the fire-light playing on the faces of the tired and anxious men'.

On the next day everyone reached Cuttack, being greatly aided by the Group Captain in command of a nearby airfield. The journey was over a very bad road, no more than a cart track, and proved for the wounded a severe test of endurance. They bore it gallantly and one Chinese hand, with a badly injured leg, apologized for his weakness in fainting by pointing to it and saying with a smile 'No meat, plenty bone'. At Cuttack the wounded went to hospital, the hale to the buildings of a local college where they were most efficiently cared for by a Mrs. C. Shaw, the only European in the town at that time.

Meanwhile the survivors of the *Indora* were also ashore. She had been the ship furthest from the enemy cruisers, and seeing the fate of the others, her Captain after an unsuccessful attempt to close the shore, stopped her and ordered the crew to the boats. This prompt action saved their lives for they 'had just pulled clear of the stern when the first salvo struck the *Indora* in the engine and boiler rooms. A second salvo seemed to be all that was required, and the ship settled down quickly. All six ships had been sunk in rather less than three-quarters of an hour.'

The Master moved to and fro picking up men from the *Autolycus* and the *Malda* until his boat held 'fifty-three persons . . . six more than her capacity'. Sail was hoisted and a course set for Chandballi, north of False Point 'where safe landings existed'. At dusk they were still some distance from land, and anchored for the night, moving on at dawn on the next day. By then the Master was in trouble with some of the shipwrecked Indian seamen from one of the other ships.

They 'refused to assist in any way' and their conduct which had become threatening, forced him to abandon his original plan and make for shore at once. This course he had been reluctant to adopt lest a rough landing should prove fatal to a Chinese hand from the *Autolycus* 'who had one of his legs almost shot away and the other . . . badly wounded'.

The boat landed safely, the unruly elements in it, who provided the only example in the records of Indian seamen failing in their duty, made off, and the rest pitched camp near the village of Panit. On the next day the Chief Officer and a small party, having unsuccessfully pursued 'the decampers', reached Rajpara where, hearing 'of their whereabouts . . . we made arrangements for them to be found and returned to Calcutta'. The Master and his men, carrying the injured Chinese hand on a makeshift stretcher, joined the Chief Officer and those with him and all presently reached Chandballi where 'the Port Officer was extremely hospitable' and was able to send them to Calcutta where they met with the survivors of the *Malda*, who had been taken to that city by train from Cuttack.

The loss of life in this ship and the others would have been very much smaller had the crews been given time to enter the boats before the warships opened fire; but 'no opportunity was given to abandon ship and no warning signal was made by the enemy'.

The day after the *Malda* and *Indora* were sunk by Japanese cruisers off Calcutta, the *Fultala*, a new cargo vessel which had left the slips only two years before, was sunk by a Japanese submarine off Ceylon. The enemy was especially active that spring in the waters of the Indian Ocean and the Bay of Bengal, for he was striving like all aggressors to win victory quickly. He failed and the war went on through that grim summer when, with Malaya and Burma lost, the eastern bastions were down and it seemed that nothing could prevent the successful invasion of India. Yet for the Company there was a pause of longer span than that which had occurred after the fall of Rangoon. Not until 9th September 1942 was another ship lost. On that day the *Haresfield* met her fate.

In March that year she had rendered good service to the Cunard Company's vessel *Georgic*, which was being towed by a tug to Karachi. In the Red Sea the *Haresfield* took over the task from the tug which was in difficulties owing to the heavy weather, and brought the *Georgic* safely to port after a voyage of twenty-three days, 'the longest tow on record for a ship of this size.' On 9th September the *Haresfield*, on passage from Aden to Calcutta in ballast, was off the island of Socotra, when, in a choppy, confused sea, she received two torpedoes, a third exploding 800 feet short of her. The second was fired nearly two hours after the first and was a *coup de grâce*, for by then the vessel's stern 'was completely out of the water'. Captain T. E. C. Earl had already given the order to abandon ship and all on board got away in four lifeboats and a raft. 'A strong easterly wind was running at the time and an adverse wind for making Socotra', so the Captain 'advised the boats to sail in a northerly direction hoping we could make the Arabian, Mekran or Sind coasts'. During the night the boats parted company.

No. 1 reached Karachi on the morning of 23rd September, after a voyage of fourteen days, a very remarkable feat of seamanship on the part of the Chief Officer, Mr. G. E. Hopkins. All on board were sent to hospital suffering from exposure and exhaustion. No. 3 boat, under the Captain, was rescued two days later when within a day's sail of the same port, by the s.s. *Jalaratna* of the Scindia Steam Navigation Company. Being outward bound, she took them to

Aden. No. 6 boat's company were picked up after six days by an Arab dhow and brought into Muscat; those in No. 5 boat also eventually reached Muscat. The tale of their adventures has been told by Mr. M. G. Brookfield, the *Haresfield's* Second Officer. It reads like the adventures of a hero in a novel of Stevenson or Ballantyne.

Brookfield was in his bath when the first torpedo struck the *Haresfield*, and ran on deck clad only in a towel to meet 'blasts of hot air and a rush of water'. Returning for clothes he found his cabin wrecked and fresh water, which he was presently to long for so fiercely, 'dripping out of the tank'. He returned to the deck wearing this time a steel helmet and 'a rather insubstantial dressing gown' with a 'panic bag' slung over his shoulder. He saw his men into their boat and then entered it himself, cast off, and presently transferred with six others to No. 5 boat which had 'no one experienced in charge'. There were twenty all told on board, sixteen Indians and four Europeans; among them were the wireless operator and two Naval gunners. The mast was hoisted 'and then the mainsail, reefed to its maximum . . . The boat was . . . tossing wildly by this time and, spray-soaked as we were, it was a relief to get more or less heading north with the strong wind and breaking seas on our port quarter. We had agreed to make for the Arabian coast.' Long before dawn they were alone and remained thus for eleven days.

At first the weather continued stormy and the tiller broke. It was mended by a length from the boat-hook hacked off with an axe. Bill, the Cockney gunner, 'took over the thankless task of issuing the food and water, and most fairly and expertly carried on throughout—both afloat and on land'. A tin of cigarettes found in Brookfield's 'panic bag' lasted nine days, the ration on the first being one cigarette each, dwindling daily until the ninth, when it was 'half a cigarette to ten men, a mere puff and pass on'. The nights were cold, the days very hot. The first were a great trial to the Indian crew who huddled two and a half men to a blanket, under 'the canvas hood and screens fitting over the portion of the boat forward of the mast . . . a Godsend'. During daylight hours their places were taken by the four Europeans who could shelter there from the fierce sun, 'the lapping of the water on the bows our constant music. The last hour . . . before sunset was the nicest part of the day. We would cool off and discuss rations'. Of these, fortunately, there were enough. 'We fed quite well, the biscuits were really tasty. There were milk tablets and two dozen tins of condensed milk and some chocolate, but water caused some anxiety. After a week I cut the ration down to two dippers a day and this caused some dissatisfaction. Some of the Indians put forward in all honesty their outlook, which was that they should eat and drink more or less freely while the supplies lasted, and if they weren't rescued by then—well, just a shrug of the shoulders.'

Tricks at the helm were shared by Brookfield, Bill and a fireman 'who proved to be quite good'. 'Sparks' and Syd, the other gunner, after they had conquered their sea-sickness, proved by their 'never failing optimism and friendliness' to be 'very acceptable companions'.

After ten days 'Bill . . . one dawn screwed his eyes up, pointed, and said in a matter-of-fact voice "There's land over there".' It was an island 'as bare as only sand and rock can look' and, disregarding it, they went on to the mainland which at first seemed equally desolate. 'The coast was rocky, and high cliffs jutted into the sea. Then suddenly (from out of caves in the rocks as we learnt afterwards) and miraculously as it seemed to us, a dozen or so human beings materialized and after a lot of guttural exclamations and waving . . . three Arab men swam out to the boat.' They were friendly but no one could understand their speech. By signs they were induced to bring a skin half-full of water which 'tasted like what I should imagine stagnant water with a thick green scum on it would taste like'. There was, however, no salt in it and Brookfield bought it for two silver rupees.

Sail was set once more and the boat moved along the coast until nightfall when it was anchored just outside the surf. Everyone, including the man on watch, fell asleep much exhausted; but presently they all awoke together 'with the roar of breakers all round us. Dazedly we perceived that we had drifted into shoal water. The swell was curling over with big rollers so that it was already drenching us and threatening to swamp the boat.' Bill the Cockney, 'who had done some rowing on the Thames', Syd, Sparks and the Indian Tindal (boatswain's mate) 'rose magnificently to the emergency' and rowing with strength and resolution prevented 'the boat from being swept broadside on to the seas and perhaps turning turtle . . . Suddenly I felt a shock up my arm . . . from the tiller and . . . realized we had beached . . . Everyone was joyous at our deliverance.'

'Singing snatches of song and calling excitedly to one another' they set to and emptied the boat, 'fretfully tossing at the water's edge. . . . The water casks, well bunged, were floated off and rolled up the beach, making it all vaguely reminiscent of smugglers, especially when someone started up with "Yo ho ho and a bottle of rum".' A fire was lit, the fuel being 'armfuls of dried and amazingly dead bushes'; clothes and even paper money were dried before its flames, and heedless of 'snufflings in the sand' made, it was presently discovered, by crabs, they all went to sleep again beneath a tent of crossed oars, sails and blankets.

The next morning they found their 'legs were a bit groggy after so many days during which they were hardly used', and to Brookfield 'as I staggered up the beach, suddenly the earth seemed to rock violently as in an earthquake . . . and it was difficult to keep my balance. This soon wore off but it was most startlingly vivid and real at the time'.

The shipwrecked men enjoyed their first hot meal, 'grilled crab' next morning, and presently 'we discovered our "Man Friday".' He proved to be 'a man on a camel near a dried-up river bed where it cut through high, rocky cliffs. After a while he approached and there he was. Sayad to us, a true and faithful friend who guided us and helped us in our trek to . . . Sangara, the village by the sea'. Sayad led them to a well and after they had drunk deeply they set off up the cliffs on to 'fairly level ground'. The march 'seemed interminable. . . . Each slight rise ahead would be eagerly reached only to see another in front of us, a series of monotonous, sandy waves.' Brookfield, whose shoes were falling to pieces, found himself envying Syd in his heavy marching boots. Water was the never-absent problem. 'It was difficult to transport . . . one bucket half full and slung on the boat-hook was the load of two of the seamen, and as well there was my flask and a bottle full.'

That evening they camped by some rocks, tired, thirsty and disappointed because 'we didn't know really how far we would have to go to reach anywhere habitable'. Their leader lay 'watching the stars and the bright moon through an atmosphere so pure as to make everything crystal clear'. The following morning 'we resumed our journey back', for they had decided to stay by the coast where at least there was a well, when 'we joyously spotted Sayad plodding behind his camel. . . . Soon he was among us, a wise, knowing smile on his tanned face.' He suggested that Brookfield, since he was almost barefoot, should ride his camel. Brookfield did so and discovered to his personal satisfaction why that animal has been called the ship of the desert. It is 'for its not unpleasant swaying motion as it plods along'. After an encounter with 'two mounted Arabs . . . their curved knife-sheaths . . . ornately decorated with beaten silver', the party at length reached Sayad's house, 'a few over-hung openings in the side of a wadi'. Here they met his two wives and three children and here they spent the night delighting their hostesses with a present of biscuits, and receiving in exchange 'a lovely piece of cooked fish and a little warm milk' from a goat.

The next day they reached the village of Sangara under the guidance of Sayad, Brookfield riding upon the camel 'in grand style, having draped the remnants of my dressing gown around my head and straightened my cap over it'. The most inspiring sight which met their eyes was a small dhow anchored off shore and a bundle of dates, 'and did we tuck in, flies and sand notwithstanding'. Sayad was paid off, departing with twenty rupees and the assurance that he was 'a fine, honest and helpful gentleman'.

Negotiations with the captain and owner of the dhow, one Hassan by name, were prolonged, but in the end successful, and he agreed to take them all to Muscat for 200 rupees. They boarded his vessel and set off. The next few days, though food and water were still short, were pleasant enough; the breeze was steady from the south-east and the dhow glided smoothly and rapidly through the water. The captain and his crew of two ate nothing but a little dried fish and rock salt, their one luxury being coffee which they made in an old pot above a fire held in the hollow of a turtle's shell. Once they caught a fish 'honestly, the finest tasting fish I have ever eaten' and there was a delay of twelve hours at a little village where the ship-wrecked mariners were displayed to the elders, grave men in white robes, and Brookfield expressed in writing the gratitude of all for the hospitality given to them.

Though space was precious on the dhow which was but thirty-five feet long, there was room to stretch the limbs at length and dream of 'all the good things we would eat when we got back to civilization'. The breeze held, the water gurgled at the bows, the helmsman, a young Arab, howled interminable love-songs 'to the long-suffering moon', and in due course they reached the 'land of the flying things', a small outpost of the Royal Air Force at Ras-el-Hadd where an emergency landing ground had been built. Their hardships and troubles were at last at an end.

Made welcome and taken to a mess tent where 'we had a lovely meal of bully beef and mashed potatoes followed by prunes and rice', they waited a few days longer and were then transported by the Civil Engineer of the air strip to Muscat in his power-driven dhow, and arrived there, 'every-one in good health and of good cheer'. The Indians were billeted in a hotel, the Europeans in the local hospital and made free of the Royal Air Force mess. Here Brookfield, Sparks, Bill and Syd supplemented the huge meals provided by slices of bread spread with tinned butter and raspberry jam, finding themselves able to consume a pound of jam a head for supper together with 'bread and sardines or dates which we still liked'.

The adventure ended at Karachi to which port they were taken in a China coaster, to return once more to the bombs, torpedoes, and machine-gun fire of civilization. They were overjoyed to learn 'that every single person from the *Haresfield* was safe and sound'.

The Company rejoiced with Brookfield and his gallant band. It had little cause for rejoicing, however, when the next of its ships went down. The *Tilawa* had been employed on a number of coastal voyages until November 1940 when she had been transferred to the Bombay–Africa service as a passenger vessel. On 20th November 1942 she cleared Bombay with 6,472 tons of cargo and mail, and 912 passengers, of whom seventeen were European. The ship had on board nine lifeboats, twenty-five rafts and a motor lifeboat, all of which had been carefully tested and checked before sailing. Once at sea, boat drill was carried out frequently and Captain F. Robinson, her Commander, personally inspected all life-saving gear and made certain through his officers that everyone on board knew what to do if the ship were torpedoed.

Three days later, very early in the morning in bright moonlight, 'a violent explosion' shook the ship. 'Not knowing whether the vessel had struck a floating mine or had been torpedoed,' Captain Robinson reported, 'but realizing that the position of the explosion meant that the vessel was not in immediate danger of sinking, I had every hope of proceeding and saving the ship. Unfortunately, the deck passengers crowded onto the boat-deck and saloon-deck before the wardens were able to take up their stations. They swarmed into the boats and many jumped overboard.' The shock for them had been too great, and 'from the very first (they) were out of control and were climbing into boats regardless of numbers as they were being lowered'. Summing up the situation, the Captain immediately ordered the engines to be stopped, while the Chief Officer sought to discover the whereabouts and extent of the damage. Almost at once the Chief Engineer reported that his engines were undamaged and asked for orders. The Captain told him that it was his intention to get under way again as soon as the rafts and boats were clear of the propellers. The ship could then be turned and all who had thus taken precipitately to the water would be brought on board again. In the meantime, very strenuous efforts were being made to control the situation; but the boats were overloaded and those in the water had not unhooked the falls, which added to the general confusion. 'The ladder leading to the motor-boat,' recalls one eye-witness, 'reminded one of a "fly paper" covered with flies, the motor-boat itself was then in mid-air but, unfortunately, someone allowed the after-fall to run out with the result that the boat went hurtling into the water, end on . . . throwing out the occupants in all directions.' In an attempt to go to the rescue of those already in the water clinging to rafts, an officer climbed down one of the ladders, but found that it had broken off twenty feet short of the water. He jumped for a hanging fall, down which he slid, 'much to the detriment of my hands', entered the water and was almost at once struck a heavy blow on the head by one of the fall blocks. This dazed him and he did not recover full control over his senses until picked up by the boat in the charge of the Third Officer. 'Although the sea was glassy, there was a very considerable swell . . . and this greatly impeded . . . efforts made to save life.'

Such, then, was the general situation of the *Tilawa* and her company about two o'clock on that moon-drenched November morning. The ship, though down by the head, was still afloat and seemed likely to remain so, but around her a confused assembly of boats and rafts were bobbing up and down, crowded with unhappy passengers. Slowly the control, lost in the first wild rush to the boats of the deck passengers, was being regained, when a second heavy explosion occurred. This time there could be no doubt. The ship had not hit a mine, but had herself been hit by torpedoes. Under the impact of this mortal blow, the *Tilawa* reeled heavily to port, was unable to right herself and sank in two minutes. 'All persons remaining on board jumped or were thrown into the water and made for rafts or boats as best they could.' All this time Mr. E. B. Duncan, the First Radio Officer, was at his post, transmitting S O S messages, of which the last broke off abruptly in the middle as he went down with the ship. His gallant sacrifice was not in vain. The distress calls had been picked up and the cruiser H.M.S., *Birmingham* was on the way to the rescue.

In the meantime, scenes of tragedy and comedy played themselves out as the dawn climbed slowly up the sky. The Captain and the Chief Officer, having shaken hands as the water reached them on the bridge, were swept into the sea but succeeded eventually in climbing on to a raft. While on it, the Captain saw one of the first-class passengers 'come up through the depths'. He had been washed into the Officers' bathroom from which he had been unable to extricate himself until the ship was well below the surface, 'a miraculous escape. With a badly injured collar-bone, a left arm useless, with trousers sucked off (in the pockets were thousands of pounds' worth of jewellery . . .), and his weight of seventeen stone, the difficulty I had getting him on to a small raft can be imagined, all the more so when the poor fellow almost choked with laughter after I had observed that a soft, wet, slippery, big, bare posterior was not conducive to good handling'.

Presently the Captain succeeded in trans-shipping to 'a damaged collapsible boat . . . half full of water' with thirty-eight men and one woman, 'all of them in an injured condition' on board. Captain Robinson set the sail, restored order on board and then, for the third time, transferred himself to another craft. Like the one which he had left, it was a collapsible boat, but this one contained forty-three women and one man. The women had recovered from their fright and shewed deep appreciation of the harassed Captain's efforts to help them. These included the placing of a bucket in a screened-off portion of the bows and this occasioned 'great merriment'. For a whole day the survivors drifted about in touch with each other and watched by unnumbered sharks swimming 'a foot or two below the surface'. Utterly exhausted, the Captain was dozing in his crowded boat when someone shouted in his ear something about an object flying away to the south. 'I forgot my sunburn and stiffness,' he records, 'and grabbed the binoculars. To my amazement I discerned a small plane flying eastward.' It was a Swordfish carried by H.M.S. *Birmingham* and at 8.45 p.m. that evening she arrived on the scene and began her work of rescue. 'I was at sea myself for over twenty years,' writes one of the survivors, picked up that evening, 'but never in my life have I ever seen such wonderful seamanship as that shewn by the officers and men of H.M.S. *Birmingham*." Altogether she picked up 661 survivors and brought them back to Bombay whither they arrived on 27th November.

Four days earlier the last of the Company's ships to be lost in 1942 met her end. The *Cranfield*, when steaming on a north-westerly course along the west coast of India, was hit by two torpedoes, of which the second destroyed her engines and killed a number of the engine-room staff. Those on board took to boats and rafts and were presently taken in tow by a number of fishing canoes which eventually brought them in the afternoon to Varkala village and a beach 'crowded with Indians and palm trees'. It belonged to the State of Travancore and the authorities did all they could to help, 'being very kind and considerate' and making 'anxious enquiries as to our comfort'.

So ended the sinkings for 1942. Next year was one of hard fighting at sea and of slow but certain Allied recovery. The power of the Japanese Navy was first curbed and then broken. The course of events is reflected in the tale of sinkings. In 1943 the Company lost only two vessels, both of them converted troopships, and of these, one, the *Santhia*, was sunk in Calcutta harbour when, on 6th November, she caught fire and capsized at No. 3 Garden Reach Jetty. The *Santhia* had been engaged for two years in the business of carrying troops up the Persian Gulf to Basrah and up the Red Sea to Suez. When fire broke out in the troops' baggage in No. 2 hold, there was a big complement of West Africans on board, but none was lost. For two years she blocked a valuable berth and was an object of interest to all who passed up and down the river. On 1st April 1945 the work of salvage began and proved one of the most difficult tasks ever attempted. It was very hard for divers to maintain themselves in position owing to the strong tides of the Hooghly, of which the water was so muddy that all vision was totally obscured. The *Santhia* was canted over at an angle of ninety-three degrees and, if pulled upright, would either crush herself or the jetty. The first operation was to remove her ballast, the silt of the river which had accumulated inside her hull and her entire superstructure. This was accomplished in four months by divers unable to work more than one at a time. It was next necessary to turn the ship 'deck side up'. A concrete wall 'capable of withstanding a horizontal pull of two thousand tons' was built 'to act as an anchor block against the pull to be exerted and the quay was strengthened with steel sheet piling'. Bolted to the uppermost part of the vessel were twenty thirty-foot high A-frames of Oregon pine. They were connected to twenty hand winches and by October all were in operation, being worked manually by 150 coolies. The ship came over almost imperceptibly, for it required 180 turns of a winch to move the top of the A-frames a distance of one and a half inches. These tactics were eventually successful and, by the end of November, the *Santhia* was upright and half afloat. She was eventually successfully towed into the King George V dock, and her bell, rescued from its muddy grave, presented to the Children's School of Bogong.

The *Nirpura* was, properly speaking, not a converted troopship but a vessel fitted to carry mules, horses and donkeys. Of these she had 667 of the first and 35 each of the second and third on board when on 3rd March, in convoy from Durban, she was torpedoed. The officers and crew took to the boats and rafts, one of them, who was asleep in his bunk at the time, putting his hand out to touch the ship's side and experiencing 'the ghastly feeling of my hand grasping space. The ship's side . . . had been blown away.' Some of the men on board had fallen into the sea and, since it was dark and they had no lights attached to their lifebelts, could not be found. 'All we could do,' reported one of them, 'was to put one hand on a small buoyancy tank which allowed us to keep our balance but gave us no support. Next morning, with about eight of us left, the only thing visible was a raft with one man on it. I now felt too weak to swim to it so I just kept one hand on the tank. During the morning we lost three others. I did not see them go but I kept a good eye on Mr. Karna, our Indian Engineer, who had the sense to say every time he had cramp. What looks like a calm sea from a ship seems like a storm when you are swimming in it.' Having been in the water about eighteen hours, these men were eventually picked up by a trawler. Those in the boats were more fortunate, and when dawn came, watched the *Nirpura* sink. She shut up like a pair of scissors, bow and stern meeting, as she plunged beneath the waves. They were picked up by an Argentine steamer which, being neutral, was burning lights.

By 1944, though Japan was to hold out well into the summer of the next year, she was a defeated nation. She had been driven back and back, her fortress chain of islands had been pierced, and, though Singapore was still in her hands, her power to carry on the war at sea had been gravely crippled. As in the previous year, the Company had to deplore the loss of only two ships. The first of these was the *Surada*, a cargo and passenger vessel. She was one of a convoy of twenty ships on passage from Colombo to Aden. The convoy had been dispersed off Bombay, each ship being ordered to proceed to her destination in accordance with individual routing instructions. On 26th January, about forty miles north-east of the Island of Socotra, not very far from where, two years before, the *Haresfield* had gone down, she was struck by a torpedo. All on board were able to take to the boats and row clear of the ship, which was sinking very rapidly. She went down in five minutes, 'blowing her whistle'. Soon after she had disappeared, the submarine surfaced and made for the boats. The sea was littered with tea chests and wreckage, and among these they took cover lest the submarine should be tempted to follow the infamous and by then well-established practice of shelling the boats of torpedoed merchantmen.

The boat in charge of the Second Engineer, less fortunate than the rest, was discovered by the submarine and ordered alongside. To the astonishment of its occupants, however, the two officers who spoke with them confined themselves to a number of routine questions concerning the ship's cargo and destination, asked whether there were any wounded on board and whether food and water were plentiful. On being told that they were, the officer then gave the distance to the nearest land and the course which should be steered. One of the men in the boat, a German-speaking Dutch Naval officer, said that those who had accosted them were undoubtedly Germans, whereas the hands who had been fending off the boat from the side of the submarine were undoubtedly Japanese. The loss of the *Surada* was, according to her Captain, 'a copy-book·sinking'. As soon as the submarine had disappeared, the boats were taken in tow by the motor-boat and a course was shaped for Socotra. To save petrol, sails were hoisted in the boats, and the strange appearance of three small ships with sails set accompanied by a fourth which had no sails but still contrived to keep up with its companions, attracted the attention of the Chief Officer of the passing *Darro*. He had sighted them early in the morning and had at first mistaken them for fishing vessels. They were all picked up and taken back to Aden.

The last of the Company's ships to feel the bolt of war was the little *Baroda*, the ship which had saved so many unhappy men, women and children from the clutches of the Japanese when they invaded Burma. On 14th April 1944, she was destroyed, not by bomb, mine or torpedo, but by fire when berthed in Bombay. Mr. S. G. James, the Chief Officer, had just completed the task of paying off the crew when it was reported to him that a ship, the *Fort Stikine*, was on fire. He ran for the bridge and saw that she was, indeed, blazing. He battened down the hatches on the *Baroda*, and ordered fire hoses to be rigged. Then he ran down the gangway to telephone for the Master, who was ashore. On the way he met the Cargo Superintendent of the Company, who gave him the grim information that there were explosives on board the *Fort Stikine*. To emphasize these words 'the first explosion occurred and parts of No. 4 shed and debris' fell upon them. James returned to the *Baroda* which was 'surging heavily up and down against the dock wall', and found a quantity of hay on the poop on fire. By then the crew had abandoned the ship and there were but four men left on board. All moorings had carried away but James and the Chief Engineer with difficulty released the windlass brake and thus let go both bow anchors. Together with the Fourth Engineer and the Purser, they then tried to fight the fire which had by then broken through on the poop. But before they could do so effectively, it had reached the ship's armaments and the ammunition began to explode. They still, however, continued their efforts, seeking to set up a portable emergency motor pump. While doing so, a second explosion took place on the *Fort Stikine*, blowing the ship across the end of the next berth and plunging the whole neighbourhood into darkness for the space of ten minutes. This explosion wrecked the *Baroda* whose Chief Engineer fell unconscious beneath a stokehold ventilator and appeared to be severely injured. The three on board with him tried without success to lower him into the water, 'but were unable to do so on account of obstructions and our own physical weakness.' By now the *Baroda* was blazing from stem to stern, and those still on board were compelled to abandon ship. Soon afterwards they met with a rescue party, and the Fourth Engineer led it back, but by that time the flames were so fierce that they were unable to approach.

Such was the end of the *Baroda*, and of the Company's losses, save for the *Takliwa*, wrecked on the Nicobar Islands in October 1945, and the *Neuralia*, mined on the eve of V.E. Day. Though they did not know it at the time, death's grim tally was at last exhausted. More than a year was still to pass before the unconditional surrender of Japan made final victory an accomplished fact; but though during that time large numbers of the Company's fleet were employed in the offensive which ended with the recapture of Burma and Malaya, none of them was lost. To tell in detail the story of their journeys, it would be necessary to describe both the second Burma and the second Malaya campaign. Let it suffice that the first required hard fighting before the fall of Rangoon gave Burma, for a short time, back to the Empire and the second was over almost before it had begun. In both the part played by the majority of the Company's fleet involved was the same. Troopers like *Egra, Ekma, Ellenga, Ethiopia, Rajula, Dilwara,* and, of course, the almost ubiquitous *Nevasa,* carried the fighting men and the stores; cargo boats such as the *Itria, Itola, Itaura,* brought supplies; hospital ships such as the *Vita* and the *Vasna* were in constant attendance. The *Rajula* was fitted out as an ambulance transport, having on board a medical staff and beds for casualties, the remaining accommodation being retained for ordinary trooping purposes. In this capacity she made several voyages between Arakan and India, but neither claimed nor received the protection accorded under the Geneva Convention to an ordinary hospital ship. The *Warina,* acting as a Naval Collier, was one of the convoy destined for the invasion of the Malacca Straits—Operation Zipper, as it was called. Another was the Royal Air Force Depot Ship, the *Manela,* whose role was one of the strangest of her wartime career. She sailed from Singapore, leading fifty Landing Craft Tanks and other miscellaneous small craft, and looking 'rather like a mother duck with all her ducklings cruising across the ocean'. Fortunately the Japanese surrendered before it became necessary to storm the beaches, and the *Manela* finished the war at Saletar, whither she brought elements of the Royal Air Force to set themselves up once more on an airfield from which they had been driven three years before.

It must not be supposed that because the voyages of these ships are passed over in a few lines they were not arduous, protracted and perilous. They were. But with every mile the ships steamed, with every horizon they pursued, they were urged on by the wind of victory. It was a potent blast, fanning the ardour of the tired men on board them to kindle to bright flame once more a spirit, never extinct but smouldering dully, pertinaciously, through long years of seeming frustration and wasted effort. To all the men in all those ships, the joy of victory was granted, but to the companies of one or two, the *Vasna* and the *Dunera*, was given the privilege to behold with their own eyes the enemy in his most bitter hour of defeat.

The *Vasna* was the first of all British hospital ships to arrive in Kure, the port for Tokyo, 'and the first to go alongside in a Japanese port after the cessation of hostilities', records Mr. C. D. Scott, who had served on her as a Supply Officer since February 1942. After a period of rest following her service at the landings on Ramree and Cheduba in January 1945, the *Vasna* had sailed to South Africa and Ceylon. She then left for the Far East to join the Pacific Fleet, taking to their homes on the way 'a full complement of Australian and New Zealand' wounded and sick. She reached Japan about a month after the surrender. The scene as she entered Yokohama, as Scott depicts it, was remarkable. A great fleet, composed for the most part of American warships, stretched in unbroken lines across the twelve miles of Tokyo Bay, interspersed with the hulks of sunken Japanese men of war. 'As *Vasna* sailed through this vast armada to her allotted berth in Yokohama inner harbour, one could not help but feel sad to think that so many of our countrymen and Allies had not been spared to witness this scene of triumph.' A reception camp for rescued prisoners of war had been established by the Americans on the dockside, and from its rejoicing, but debilitated, occupants the *Vasna* made up the last and most remarkable of her passenger lists. She took on board all not of American or Canadian nationality who were unfit to travel except on a hospital ship. The men were made as comfortable as possible and stocks of chocolates, sweets, beer and cigarettes, generously contributed by the officers and men of the British Pacific Fleet who had themselves gone short in order to supply them, were distributed throughout the ship. In due course she sailed away and, avoiding typhoons, brought her passengers at long last safely back to civilization.

A few months later the *Dunera* arrived in Japan on her last voyage before resuming her normal trooping duties. She had on board the Commanding-General and the Headquarters Staff of part of the Forces of Occupation, together with some 2,000 British and Indian troops.

Let this record of the adventures of the Company's ships in the Far East during four years of disaster, dogged perseverance and final triumph close with the words set down at the time by the Commander of the *Manela* as she sailed into Madras with a full complement on board of Indian soldiers returning from captivity. 'We made a grand entry into the harbour; all the ships were dressed in honour of our prisoners and they all blew their whistles in greeting.' It was the end of the journey for them as it was for all the crews of the ships belonging to the British India Steam Navigation Company. They had shewn fortitude in peril, resolution in distress, joy and compassion in victory.

9

RECONSTRUCTION

'. . . tomorrow, you will see her sail . . .'
The Wanderer—John Masefield

The war in Europe dragged its slow length along until in the spring of 1945 a series of piecemeal capitulations ended in the general and unconditional surrender of Germany. In the East the finish of Japan was not so prolonged. She received her quietus with dramatic violence when on 6th and 9th August atomic bombs fell on Hiroshima and Nagasaki. By then the strain had become insupportable for the enemy and very grievous for the Allies. How grievous can be judged by examining the record of losses in men and vessels suffered by but one of the many shipping enterprises of which the Merchant Navy is composed.

On 3rd September 1939, the British India Steam Navigation Company possessed 103 vessels, fifty-five of them passenger and forty-eight cargo, of a gross tonnage of 801,343 tons. By 15th August 1945 fifty-one of them, of a gross tonnage of 351,756 tons, had been lost by the action of the enemy or other cause. They had met their end at every stage of the war and every part of the world. Off the coasts of

Greece and Cyrenaica, of Algeria and Sicily, beneath the grey North and the bright South Atlantic, off Arabia and Malaya and Burma, in the Pacific Ocean and in the Indian lie their honoured bones. They were the victims of mine and torpedo, of bomb and shell, and they took with them to the deep 1,083 officers and men. To these casualties in ships and men may be added those sustained among the vessels owned by other concerns but managed by the Company on behalf and at the orders of the Ministry of War Transport. Of these ships, seventy-two in number belonging to eleven nationalities, sixteen were lost. Among the officers and men on board them were many of the Company's employees.

It will be perceived that the Company lost almost exactly one half of the vessels in its possession at the outbreak of war. Such a high rate of casualties might well have proved fatal. Instead, true to the example of its founder and strong in the tradition which he inaugurated, its spirit has remained unbroken, its determination unimpaired. Even before the war was over a programme of replacement had been set in train, which by January 1947 had brought twenty-four new ships into service. Many, such as the *Chyebassa*, the *Chupra* and the *Chanda*, the *Pachumba*, the *Pundua* and *Padana*, were voyaging in Eastern waters before Japan surrendered. Immediately the fighting ended, eighteen more vessels were ordered from such fine ship-builders as Alexander Stephen & Sons Limited, Barclay, Curle & Company Limited, both of Glasgow, and Swan, Hunter & Wigham Richardson Limited, of Wallsend-on-Tyne. Eight of these are passenger ships and two of them are now completed. They are the *Kampala* and her sister ship, the *Karanja*, both 500 feet long and engined by single-reduction turbines developing nearly 9,000 horsepower producing a speed of sixteen and a half knots.

Three motor ships, the *Dumra*, to replace the ship of that name lost during the war, the *Dwarka* and the *Dara* have been built for the Bombay-Persian Gulf Service. They are motor ships with a speed of fourteen knots. Calcutta and ports further east are to be served by the *Sirdhana*, the *Sangola* and a third, all twin-screw vessels with the same speed as the *Dumra* and, like the other two classes, with wide space for refrigerated stores.

Nineteen cargo vessels have already been built and nine more are building. Among them is the 'P' class of seven vessels, the *Obra* and *Okhla*, all of twelve knots, and the *Urlana* and *Umaria*. There is, too, the *Carpentaria* which, when completed, will be a motor ship of 10,500 tons with 100,000 cubic feet of refrigerated space.

Such, in briefest outline, is the programme which is now being fulfilled. It has throughout followed one general principle. Each ship, or rather each class of ship, must be specially adapted to the needs of the special trade—passenger, cargo, or a combination of both—upon which she is to be employed. Each vessel carries the most modern devices available to ensure the safety and comfort of all on board including the crew whose accommodation has been made a matter of careful concern. The problem of what life-saving equipment is most suitable—important in all ships but particularly in those transporting large numbers of unberthed passengers—has been specially studied and the correct conclusion, it is hoped, drawn from the experiences of six years of war.

But the varied equipment, the spacious holds, the modern engines, the numerous and carefully planned improvements, are not the only assets of these new and splendid ships. They will possess as well something not so tangible but more lasting, a tradition and a pride created by those who have

M.S. CHANDA

S.S. KAMPALA

gone before them and whose honoured names several of them bear. Far back beyond the limits of the longest voyage go their predecessors—back to the first creaking paddle-steamer bringing the soldiers of the Queen to what was then the wide Empire of India. Nearly a hundred years have passed since the *Cape of Good Hope* dropped anchor in the Hooghly and her sisters began their voyaging to the forest-fringed ports of Burma and the islands of Malaya; but the spirit and intention of service then made manifest for the first time has endured to this day. It grew and burgeoned as the years went by and paddles yielded to propellers, and the soldiers on the troop-decks replaced a scarlet tunic by a khaki shirt, and the passengers in the saloons exchanged strapped trousers or a crinoline for a tropical suit or a two-piece, and motorcars and Bren guns ousted dog-carts and Gatlings from the holds.

Twice in its existence has the Company endured the heavy test of a world war, and twice it has emerged triumphant. The second time the ordeal was peculiarly severe for the struggle was so prolonged and the losses so heavy that the crews of its ships, had they been less staunch, might well have quailed. They did not. European and Indian seaman alike—courage takes no account of colour—from the captain on the bridge with thirty years of service behind him to the Indian seaman in the fo'c'sle on his first voyage, bore with stout hearts all the manifold shocks of war. In peace-time the Merchant Navy is only too often forgotten or taken for granted by a people intent on their own affairs. In war-time it is otherwise; for then the debt owed is plain and becomes plainer with every new rationing regulation, every new restriction. These serve as ungentle reminders that Great Britain is an island and that those who dwell thereon depend in peace-time for the amenities, in war-time for the necessities, of life upon a few thousand of their fellow countrymen who sail the Seven Seas. Not the least among them are the officers and men of the British India Steam Navigation Company. They performed a double duty, for the greater part of the ships in which they sailed carried at one time or another either food and supplies to Britain or stores, equipment and men to her armies in the many theatres of war. Braving all the perils provoked by nature or man which can beset a sailor at sea, some had good fortune and when the war was over could report, in the laconic words of the Captain of the *Masula*, that 'raiders, submarines and bombers confined their attention strictly to other ships'. Others had not and suffered wounds and injuries and long days and nights of hardship in open boats. Still others, unflinching, met their fate and perished gallantly with the ship that bore them.

To all these men the new crews on the new ships owe a great debt. For those who served through the Second World War have by the sacrifice of many and the deeds of all enhanced the repute of a great name and added a golden page to the story of the sea. That is why the ships now setting forth along 'the wet road heaving, shining' in all the strength and comeliness of youth will carry within them, beneath the Company's flag, not only the goods and products by the export of which this country must rebuild her strength, but also a tradition of devotion, endurance and faith which is above the peculiar treasure of kings.

APOLOGIA

Whilst every care has been exercised in compiling the list of Prisoners of War, yet these records may possibly not include all who were unfortunate enough to fall into the hands of the enemy. In many instances records obtained from other countries were very incomplete and, in some cases, ships were sunk without any knowledge becoming available as to the ultimate fate of those on board. Similarly, in the case of Honours Awards and Casualties, every effort has been made to make the lists complete, but their accuracy and completeness cannot be guaranteed, and regret is expressed for any errors or omissions which inadvertently may have occurred.

APPENDICES

1

ROLL OF HONOUR

Officers and Men who lost their lives at sea
due to enemy action

Men
It's a sunny pleasant anchorage
Is kingdom come . . .
Port of Many Ships—John Masefield

EUROPEANS

s.s. *ASKA*

J. A. W. Elrick	*Third Engineer*
C. J. Green	*Fourth Engineer*
A. B. Aitken	*Junior Engineer*
T. Toole	,, ,,
J. Martin	,, ,,
R. D. Easton	,, ,,

s.s. *CALABRIA*

Captain D. Lonie	*Commander*
R. W. Macdonald	*Chief Officer*
L. H. White	*Second Officer*
H. F. A. Berry	*Cadet*
L. C. Norris	,,

E. Shone	*Purser*
L. Butler	*Surgeon*
A. R. Masson	*Chief Engineer*
J. E. Benson	*Second Engineer*
C. Paterson	*Third Engineer*
D. Rae	*Fourth Engineer*
S. A. Wallis	*Junior Engineer*
D. C. Jenkins	,, ,,
R. O. Duncan	,, ,,
A. Sterling	,, ,,

S.S. *CHILKA*

K. M. Feast	*Second Officer*
G. B. Hodges	*Third Officer*
J. B. Kerr	*Fourth Engineer*

M.S. *DOMALA*

Captain W. A. Fitt	*Commander*
R. W. Peasgood	*Second Officer*
S. C. Baker	*Cadet*
C. Murray	,,
E. W. Oxspring	,,
J. McDougall	*Purser*
R. F. H. Donaldson	*Assistant Purser*
J. McGlashan	*Surgeon*
I. F. Kay	*Third Engineer*
J. Dunn	*Junior Engineer*
F. O'Hanlon	,, ,,
H. H. Morgan	,, ,,
H. S. Smith	*Quartermaster*
S. A. Hunt	*Chief Steward*
G. Abbott	*Chef*
C. Fuggle	*Baker*
Mrs. A. Elcoat	*Stewardess*
Mrs. V. H. Wymer	,,

M.S. *DUMANA*

George Reid Tait	*Third Officer*
J. C. Burton	*Second Engineer*
W. Regan	*Junior Engineer*
J. Thomson	*Electrician*

M.S. *DUMRA*

Captain W. C. Cripps	*Commander*
H. T. Graham	*Chief Engineer*
S. G. Barnes	*Junior Engineer*

S.S. *EMPIRE LIGHT*

Captain F. Dolton	*Commander*
A. Thomson	*Chief Officer*
A. E. Broadley	*Chief Engineer*
J. G. Hunter	*Second Engineer*

S.S. *ERINPURA*

E. R. Smith	*Junior Engineer*
C. McGill	,, ,,

S.S. *GAIRSOPPA*

Captain G. Hyland	*Commander*
G. D. Cummings	*Chief Officer*
C. J. Morrison	*Third Officer*
J. M. Woodliffe	*Cadet*
W. F. Dupuy	*Purser*
P. E. Fyfe	*Chief Engineer*
R. Lang	*Second Engineer*
A. P. Carmichael	*Third Engineer*
H. H. Odd	*Fourth Engineer*
W. Lucas	*Junior Engineer*

S.S. *GANDARA*

F. W. Baker	*Chief Officer*

S.S. *GARMULA*

J. L. Godfrey	*Chief Engineer*
J. W. Storey	*Second Engineer*
J. D. Walker	*Fourth Engineer*

S.S. *GOGRA*

Captain J. Drummond	*Commander*
F. R. K. Langdon	*Chief Officer*
A. N. MacTavish	*Second Officer*

T. B. Patterson	*Chief Engineer*
F. J. A. Westlake	*Second Engineer*
T. G. Ross	*Third Engineer*
J. McGeachy	*Third Engineer*

KHEDIVE ISMAIL

L. A. Lowe	*Third Engineer*
F. Simons	*Second Engineer*
J. Docherty	*Third Engineer*
T. C. Paterson	*Fourth Engineer*

s.s. *MALDA*

W. A. Davis	*Fourth Engineer*
E. Sale	*Junior Engineer*

s.s. *MANON*

A. N. Macaulay	*Second Engineer*

s.s. *MUNDRA*

J. A. Matheson	*Chief Officer*

s.s. *NARDANA*

S. H. Wright	*Third Engineer*
C. E. Miller	*Fourth Engineer*
G. W. Brain	*Junior Engineer*

s.s. *NIRPURA*

T. Scaife	*Second Engineer*
J. M. Kennedy	,, ,,

s.s. *NOWSHERA*

R. A. Philp	*Second Engineer*

s.s. *ROHNA*

G. W. Burrell	*Chief Officer*
A. C. Cranfield	*Second Officer*
J. A. Welsh	*Second Engineer*
J. Pugh	*Fourth Engineer*
J. Hulme	*Junior Engineer*

s.s. *SIR HARVEY ADAMSON*

Captain J. R. D. Weaver	*Commander*
H. Becher	*Chief Officer*
P. J. Allitt	*Second Officer*
H. Simpson	*Cadet Third Officer*
G. Wight	*Chief Engineer*
G. Patterson	*Second Engineer*
D. Bell	*Third Engineer*
A. D. Lees	*Fourth Engineer*

s.s. *TILAWA*

Captain K. S. McLennan	*Commander*
A. Frew	*Chief Officer*
P. H. Cumming	*Third Engineer*
J. S. Anderson	*Junior Engineer*
W. F. Swinton	,, ,,
H. C. Briegal	*Chef*

s.s. *WARFIELD*

G. R. Deans	*Second Engineer*

s.s. *WAROONGA*

S. Button	*Chief Engineer*
J. Paul	*Second Engineer*

s.s. *WINKFIELD*

J. Allan	*Third Engineer*

R.N.R. AND R.I.N.R.

Cadet A. V. Pumfrey (Midshipman, H.M.S. *Daring*).
Cadet R. V. N. Levinge (Sub. Lieutenant, H.M.S. *Glowworm*).
A. W. Whitfield, Second Officer (H.M.S. *Calypso*).
E. H. Smith, Chief Officer (in command, H.M.S. *Manistee*).
A. R. Gimblett, Lieutenant, R.N.R. (Missing, presumed killed in action, 2.8.40).
T. M. Mani, Third Officer (H.M.I.S. *Prabhavati*).
R. B. Davis, Second Officer (missing, presumed killed, 11.5.42).
Cadet R. A. S. Pratt (Sub. Lieutenant, H.M.S. *Dunedin*).
Captain H. T. Hudson, R.N.R. (Commodore of Convoys).

J. I. Miller, D.S.O., D.S.C., R.N.R. (H.M.S. *Salina*).
A. Sayers, R.N.R. (H.M.S. *Karanja*).
S. M. J. Mortimer, R.N.R. (H.M.S. *Karanja*).
H. H. Weeks, Cadet (Sub. Lieutenant, R.N.R.).
P. G. Cocklin, Cadet (Serving in R.A.F.).

INDIAN SEAMEN

s.s. *ASKA*

A. J. Fernandes	*General Servant*
Jeronio P. Rodrigues	*Chief Cook*
J. F. Almeida	*Troop. Storekeeper*
R. Bernardo	*Saloon Storekeeper*
Ali Ahmad x Asmat Ali	*Oilman*
Hossain Ali x Abdul	"

s.s. *BAMORA*

Joao Pinto	*General Servant*

s.s. *CALABRIA*

Fazal Bari x Reazuddin	*Serang*
Sk. Seadut x Munjoor Sk.	*First Tindal*
Abdul Aziz x Banoo	*Second Tindal*
Abdul Wahab x Sadee Sk.	*Cassab*
Umbore Ali x Toboo Sk.	*Winchman*
Chand Mian x Sudder Ali	*Seacunny*
Amjad Allee x Hakim Ali	"
Ameer Ahamode x Wazeer Ali	"
Yeacoob Allee x Eusuph Ali	"
Abdul Joralli x Molla Ganheruddin	*Lascar*
Sk. Hamid x Cader Sk.	"
Panchoo x Sk. Ismail	"
Akbar x Nizamat	"
Munzoor x Azher Sk.	"
Usman Sk. x Ozob Sk.	"
Abdul x Amjad	"
Sadeck x Nadir Sk.	"
Ahmad Newaz x Nobee Newaz	"
Teetoo Molla x Abbas Molla	"
Ramez Ali x Meher Ali	"

Mohd. Idris x Abdul Ghafur	*Lascar*
Wahed x Jessarabulla	,,
Abdul Hossain x Ghulam Rabbani	,,
Noor Mohamed x Bhooloo Sk.	,,
Jabedur Rahman x Majidur Rahman	,,
Asphia x Fazal Bari	,,
Abdul Mohit x Nizabber Sk.	,,
Farak Hossain x Sahebjan	,,
Sk. Ahmad x Teenoo	,,
Abdul Karim x Abdul Aziz	*Bhandary*
Abdul Maleck x Abdul Wahad	*Bhandary's Mate*
Pearoo x Bacha	*Topass*
Rathiya x Ganesh	,,
Jaya Naik x Nabu Naik	,,
Mozai Sk. x Monie Sk.	*Lascar*
Ameer Allee x Munsoor Ali	*Serang*
Luttfar Rahman x Golam Ali	*First Tindal*
Abdool Somode x Allee Meah	*Second Tindal*
Abdool Gunny x Asgar Allee	*Cassab*
Matiar Rahman x Nazir Ali	*Iceman*
Abdul Khaleque x Hashim Ali	*Lampman*
Abdul Gaffoor x Anwar Ali	*Donkeyman*
Choonoo Meah x Mon Gazi	*Oilman*
Bassa Meah x Kala Meah	,,
Raja Meah x Hyder Ali	,,
Abdus Samad x Heda Gazi	,,
Anoo Mian x Abdur Rahman	,,
Shookoor Ahmad x Qurban Ali	,,
Bela Meah x Ossie Meah	*Fireman*
Abdool Maleck x Abdul Majid	,,
Omda Meah x Hyder Ali	,,
Sona Mian x Rahim Ali	,,
Sultan Ahmode x Abdul Latiff	,,
Attore Allee x Anwar Allee	,,
Siddiq Ahmad x Chand Mian	,,
Noor Bux x Fazal Rahman	,,
Omer Meah x Abdul Hamid	,,
Khalilur Rahman x Abbas Ali	,,
Ishil Ahmad x Saddock Alee	,,
Syed Rahman x Abdul Latiff	,,
Wadil Huq x Eusuph Ali	,,
Abdul Jolil x Nazir Ali	,,
Allee Ahmode x Rofizuddin	,,

Buxsha Meah x Abdul Rahman	*Fireman*
Jalal Ahmode x Nazir Ali	,,
Ali Ahamad x Karam Ali	,,
Syed Ahmad x Olly Meah	,,
Kholill Rohman x Hasmut Allee	,,
Nabu Meah x Hasmat Allee	,,
Abdul Khair x Mofizullah	*Coal Trimmer*
Abdul Razzaque x Abdul Majid	,,
Nazir Ahmed x Rossed Ali	,,
Badsha Meah x Thanda Mian	,,
Bacha Mian x Rahamat Ali	,,
Nozoo Meah x Hamid Ali	,,
Abdul Ghani x Neamat Ali	,,
Wali Meah x Mushrafali	,,
Abdul Aziz x Kala Mian	,,
Fozlur Rahman x Ashrafali	,,
Nazoo Meah x Monoo Mian	,,
Seedick Ahmode x Saduck Ali	,,
Nou Ahmad x Hakimullah	,,
Abdul Sattar x Mon Gazi	,,
Doola Meah x Anwar Ali	,,
Worzoon x Gorib Saha	*Bhandary*
Jakhai x Khan Khan	*Bhandary's Mate*
J. Fernandes x P. Fernandes	*Butler*
Nicholas Alfanso x J. M. Alfanso	*Storekeeper*
Santan Martin	*Chief Cook and Baker*
Andy Gonslaves x J. F. Gonslaves	*Second Cook*
C. B. Alfanso x F. Alfanso	*Third Cook*
M. S. Rebello x C. Rebello	*Pantryman*
F. X. D. Almeida x C. Almeida	*Captain's Boy*
Erfan Khan x Rajab Allee	*Chief Engineer's Boy*
S. Fernandes x J. X. Fernandes	*General Servant Boy*
F. I. D'Cruz x M. D'Cruz	,,
S. R. Fernandes x C. Fernandes	,,
A. R. Fernandes x F. Fernandes	,,
Agdul Jubber x Abdul Cader	,,
Syedur Rahman x Rahim Buksh	,,
Mohamed Nokoo x Ansar Ali	*Half General Servant Boy*
Kassim Ali x Karam Ali	,, ,,
Sokoo x Kandai	*Butcher*
Mohamed Jan x Dil Md.	*Galley Scullion*
Baboo x Patram	*Topass*
Francis Davies x Martin Davis	*General Servant Boy*

L. P. Miranda x I. S. Miranda	*General Servant Boy*
Gurdit Singh	*Wireman*
Sharazool Haq	,,

Passenger Crew for the s.s. *Vasna* proceeded by the s.s. *CALABRIA*

Abdool Rahman x Md. Hossain	*Deck Serang*
Abdul Ghafur x Chand Mian	*First Tindal*
Habeeoolla x Rumjan Allee	*Second Tindal*
Abdul Jalil x Yeacoob	*Cassab*
Abdul Barrick x Ahamode Ali	*Winchman*
Secunder x Bhola Gazee	*Seacunny*
Jalal Ahamode x Mucklas Rohoman	,,
Seedick Ahamode x Mushraf Ali	,,
Munshi Mian x Md. Yeasin	*Lascar*
Sobeithoolla x Kala Meah	,,
Mozibul Haq x Abdul Barrey	,,
Muckbul Ahmed x Abdul Goffoor	,,
Fazal Rahman x Buckoor Ali	,,
Secunder Meah x Abdul Guny	,,
Abdul Khaleck x Abdul Aziz	,,
Sultan Ahmed x Bossirulla	,,
Sookor Ali x Keramat Ali	,,
Abdur Rashid x Neamat Ali	,,
Rajab Meah x Lall Meah	,,
Sultan Ahmad x Somed Ali	,,
Yaqub Ali x Omed Ali	,,
Nurual Haq x Abdul Khaleck	,,
Sobee Ahmed x Ashraf Ali	,,
Abdul Khoyer x Keramat Ali	,,
Doloo Meah x Maqbul Ali	,,
Jalal Ahmed x Muckran Ali	,,
Rajab Ali Somoroody	*Bhandary*
Musa Mian x Anwar Ali	*Bhandary's Mate*
Abdul Hassein x Moniruddin	*Seacunny*
Baladin x Boodhoo	*Topass*
Panna x Moonshi	,,
Mewa Lall x Budhoo	,,
Nanku x Merai	,,
Sultan Mian x Abdul Karim	*F. Serang*
Anwar Allee x Omer Allee	*First Tindal*
Salamatulla x Mohobuddin	*Second Tindal*
Enus Mian x Amanuddin	*Cassab*
Abdul Haque x Aslam	*Donkeyman*

Buzlur Rahman x Abdul Aziz	*Lampman*
Muslim Mian x Nasiruddin	*Iceman*
Ollyoola x Rohimoody	*Oilman*
Abdul Jabbar x Rossuen Ali	,,
Essack Mian x Aminuddy	,,
Abdul Majid x Wally Miah	,,
Habizulla x Ebadulla	*Fireman*
Islam Meah x Robinuddin Jajee	,,
Zianal Abedin x Hassan Ali	,,
Wali Mian x Erad Mian	,,
Qurban Ali x Callinuddin	,,
Salamatulla x Lall Mian	,,
Allee Meah x Robinuddy	,,
Abdul Aziz x Kobeeruddin	,,
Zulfikar x Abdul Karim	*Coal Trimmer*
Arub Allee x Someeruddin	,,
Ali Ahmed x Nokoo Mian	,,
Sheraz Meah x Keramat Ali	*Bhandary*
Nokoo Mian x Wahed Ali	*Coal Trimmer*
Sooraz Mian x Ahmad	*Oilman*
C. Correa x L. P. Correa	*Butler*
G. Gomes x D. Gomes	*Chief Cook*
Ratan Gomes x Bissoo Gomes	,, ,,
Joonun x Boodye	*Second Cook*
Modone Gomes x Hanoo Gomes	,, ,,
Kaminuddin x Rahimuddin	,, ,,
A. G. Pereira x P. F. Ferrau	*Third Cook*
Paul Charlie Gomes x Bhooban Gomes	,, ,,
Hormooz x Ahmad	*Baker*
Abdul Latiff x Sagos Mongari	*Assistant Baker*
Kamroodin x Rahimuddin	,, ,,
Mohd. Yusuf x Abdul Qadir	*Baker's Mate*
S. Baptista x P. Baptista	*Pantryman*
I. C. Gomes x R. V. Gomes	*Pantryman's Mate*
Mohamad x Jooman	*Butcher*
Hossaniee x Amir	*Assistant Butcher*
Cecil Rogers x Duncan Rogers	*Storekeeper*
M. J. Fernandes x S. Fernandes	*Assistant Storekeeper*
Nooroo Khan x Neamat Khan	*Captain's Boy*
J. Cardoze x L. Cardoze	*Chief Engineer's Boy*
Mc. Disilva x P. D'Silva	*General Servant Boy*
P. Pereira x C. Pereira	,,
J. M. Lancerdo x C. Lancerdo	,,

Francis Pereira x R. Pereira	*General Servant Boy*
P. Rebellow x R. Rebello	,,
J. P. DeCosta x J. T. D'Costa	,,
R. Countinho x A. Countinho	,,
A. Feram x F. Feram	,,
C. S. Coutinho x F. P. Coutinho	,,
Jooma x Mohamad	,,
Shew Charan x Toonoo	*Laundryman*
Bangali x Ram Lall	*Laundryman's Mate*
Kishen Lall x Kaloo	,, ,,
Hira Lall x Bahadur	*Topass*
Kassoo x Teni	*Scullion*
Lalloo x Moon Moon	*Topass*
Abdul Jubber x Romjan	*Captain's Boy*
S. Fernandes x D. Fernandes	*General Servant Boy*

s.s. *CHILKA*

Munir Ahmed x Eunos Mian	*Coal Trimmer*
Dil Mohamed	*Baker*
Ghass x Babu Lal	*Saloon Topass*

s.s. *CRANFIELD*

Amin Rohoman	*Engine Room First Tindal*
Mucklas Rahman	*Engine Room Cassab*
Raza Mian	*Oilman*
Abdool Hossein	*Fireman*
Jubber Alee	,,
Aminor Rahman	,,
Jhbul Hossain	*Coal Trimmer*
Sultan Ahmad	,,
Abdul Ghani	,,

M.S. *DOMALA*

S. K. Elahibux x Faizulla	*Tindal*
Matab x Noaz Hossain	*Winchman*
Abdul Karim x Haratulla	*Lascar*
Panchkowrie x Ezid Bux	,,
Wasoody x Derastulla	,,
Abdul Alam x Rohim Chaudhuri	,,
Tucksaid Khan x Akoo Khan	,,
Ameer Ali x Fazar Ali	,,
Ansar Ali x Syed Ali	*Lascar Boy*

Subjoo x Ramfall	*Topass*
Ramprasad x Baboo Lall	,,
Malaya x Annandi	,,
Gholam Hossain x Sk. Corban Ali	*General Servant Boy*
Ramjan Ali x Monsoor Ali	*Lampman*
Lutfa Ali x Kammaluddin	*Oilman*
Erad Mian x Mohd. Rashid	,,
Calla Meah x Akro Moody	*Coal Trimmer*
Ear Ali x Jasar Ali	,,
Tokone Meah x Ahmed Ali	*Bhandary*
Muntaz Khan x Baboo Khan	*Baker*
Gulam Rasool x Muntaz Khan	*Baker's Mate*
Monmotho Mondole x Munshi	*Chief Cook*
Ashier Gomes x Rajan Gomes	*Fourth Cook*
Patan x Porboo	*Butcher's Mate*
Shaban Khan x Jahan Khan	*General Servant Boy*
Shaik Soba x Hanoo	,,
Mahammed Yakub x Din Mahd	,,
Ersad Ali x Kurban Ali	,,
Samuel Massey	,,
Irfan Ali x Mahboob Ali	,,
Abdul Rahim x Abdul Aziz	,,
Abdul Somed x Sk. Baboo	,,
Hamid x Nazir	,,
Hooblall x Chotoo	*Topass*
Panna x Bhodhoo	,,
Chatoo x Ameer Chand	,,

Passenger Crew ex *Truenfels*, repatriated per M.S. *DOMALA*

Ishratullah x Gharibullah	*Greaser*
Romoz Allee x Fofrez Allee	,,
Anfar Ulla x Nasir Mohammad	,,
Nozaboth x Neher Ulla	*Fireman*
Watir Ulla x Alim Ulla	,,
Coorfan Ali x Mohammad Hazim	,,
Nadoo Miah x Jana Miah	,,
Ellimulla x Sollimulla	,,
Ammeer Bux x Alimoolla	,,
Anah Miah x Salamatulla	,,
Ahmadulla x Abdul Aziz	*Trimmer*
Abdur Rahman x Rowshau Ali	,,
Abdul Jubbar x Ansur Mohammed	,,

Passenger Crew ex *Lauterfels*, repatriated per M.S. *DOMALA*

Dhonoola x Sofathoolla	*Tindal*
Mahammad Mozmit x Mahammad Nassim	*Cassab*
Sikander Ulla x Rahim Ulla	*Fireman*
Sidique Ahmad x Shuzat Ali	"
Toimooscolia x Eusuphoola	"
Taher Allee x Mokaram Allee	"
Allimoolla x Rofath Oolla	"
Sharafat Ali x Ehsan Ali	"
Chian Miah x Shah Nawaz Mian	"
Bakar Mohammad x Ramiz Ulla	*Trimmer*
Appana x Papiah	*Topass*

Passenger Crew ex *Birkenfels*, repatriated per M.S. *DOMALA*

Ejat Allee x Coorfanali	*Tindal*
Jowad Allee x Cazim Meah	"
Syedulla x Wazir Mohamed	*Fireman*
Rokib Ali x Sajid Ali	*Trimmer*
Abdul Samad x Hosein Ali	*Bhandary*

Passenger Crew ex *Falkenfels*, repatriated per M.S. *DOMALA*

Tahir Allee x Sollimoolla	*Serang*
Rahimulla x Abdul Jabbar	*Tindal*
Syedoolla x Tomizoolla	*Greaser*
Woolfut Ullah x Hoyemullah	*Fireman*
Aynulla x Umbormulla	"
Nazir Ali x Mohammed Allum	"
Mossone Allee x Koy Meah	"
Kanoo Meah x Mohammed Essone	"
Rohimulla x Shoreulla	"
Ismutulla x Estimulla	"
Mohammed Hassan x Mohammed Nozobe	*Trimmer*
Muckmood Ali x Jamil Hajee	"
Mohammad Babroo x Mohammad Askar	"
Azhar Ali x Mohammad Subdar	"
Wazir Ali x Osman Ali	*Bhandary*
Nasir Ali x Hafij Ali	*Trimmer*

M.S. *DUMANA*

Munzoor Hossein x Mazahar Hossein	*Second Tindal*
Malay Sk. x Wasob Sk.	*Lascar*

Jungi x Babu Lall Baba	*Topass*
Tossore Meah x Wazidali	*Cassab*
Secunder Ali x Anfor Ali	*Oilman*
Abdul Latiff x Sk. Abdus Subhan	*Captain's Boy*
Nawab Jan x Ali Jan	*General Servant Boy*
Abdul Goffur x Hossein Buksh	"
Abdul Razack x Billoo Serang	"
Osman x Bhonda	*Baker*
Abdus Samad x Moor Mohamed	*Pantryman*
Abdul Hamid x Abdul Rohman	*Pantryman's Mate*
Golam Rahman x Golam Akhair	*General Servant Boy*
Abdul Latif Khan x Lall Khan	"
Hingoo x Mohamed Ali	*Bhandary*
Mohamed x Eusuph	*Baker's Mate*
Sk. Panchoo x Ibrahim	*General Servant Boy*
Anthony Davi	"
Asa Kirpa	*Sl. Topass*
Sooroozulla x Rashidulla	*Coal Trimmer*

M.S. *DUMRA*

Germanos Gomes	*Captain's Boy*
Jose Maria D'Almeida	*General Servant Boy*
M. R. Collasco	*Pantryman*
Caitan Fernandes	"
Manoel Louis	*Scullion*
Sk. Mohomed Mahd. Essack	*Donkeyman*
Furrack Ahmed	*Oilman*
Gafoor Sk. Hasson	"
Dajee Doolab	*Cassab*
Nana Keshav	*Seacunny*
Doolab Dhanji	"
Kesson Fackeer	"
Vallab Lalla	*Lascar*
Seeka Bhagwan	"
Doolab Narran	"
Keshav Jairam	"
Mister Idoo	*Topass*

S.S. *ERINPURA*

Foizulla x Abdul Hossein	*Dk. Serang*
Amjadali x Abdul Meah	*Second Tindal*
Sayed Ahamode x Jeanuddin	*Seacunny*

Nazir Ahmode x Abdul Karim	*Seacunny*
Abdur Rashid x Saminuddin	*Lascar*
Osman Ali x Ahmed Ali	,,
Mozoo Mian x Ayub Ali	*Lascar Boy*
Sew Pagon x Ram Dhani	*Topass*
Ram Khelwan x Ram Charan	,,
Ram Harak	,,
Shookoor x Ramjan	*Barber*
Hediat Ali x Mansoor Ali	*F. Serang*
Lall Mian x Hedawat Ali	*Donkeyman*
Mohamed x Rohomeali	*Oilman*
Abdul Juffor x Belayat Ali	,,
Nezamatali x Noor Ali	,,
Ebadur Rahman x	*Fireman*
Essack x Azamoody Bepary	,,
Abdul Sobhan x Chand Meah	,,
Hafiz Rahaman x Mangaji	,,
Arman Ali x Hasim Ali	,,
Sheroo Mian x Zohoor Mian	,,
Formuz Ali x Mohd. Itim	,,
Badsha Mian x Abdul	*Coal Trimmer*
Nur Bux x Attore Ali	,,
Abdul Azis x Mohamed Ali	,,
Asador Ali x Kajimulla	,,
Mabool Hawk x Anwar Alee	,,
Tobarack Ali x Ramjan Allee	,,
J. B. Callasco	*Butler*
J. Fernandes	*Second Cook*
P. L. Feleiro	*Baker*
J. Cardoze	*Asst. Baker*
L. F. Cardose	*Pantryman*
P. F. Almeida	*Head Waiter*
F. D'Souza	*General Servant Boy*
R. S. Costa	,,
P. P. C. DeSilva	,,
P. Swaris	,,
M. Fernandes	,,
C. Rodrigues	,,
C. DeSilva	,,
F. Souza	,,
S. Dias	,,
M. L. C. Gracias	,,
T. S. Ferrao	,,

M. P. Peris	*General Servant Boy*
P. Fernandes	*Scullion*
Tankanna	*Topass*
S. Pereira	*Troop Chief Cook*
A. DeSilva	*Troop Second Cook*
F. D'Costa	*Troop Third Cook*
A. C. Crasto	*Troop Scullion*
R. V. Viegas	*Storekeeper*

s.s. *GAIRSOPPA*

Abdool Codoos x Abdul Motaleb	*Deck Serang*
Abdul Maleck x Mustan	*Tindal*
Khoorshid Meah x Abdul Barrick	*Cassab*
Elahi Bux x Abdul Majid	*Winchman*
Abdool Mozid x Mahd. Hossone	*Seacunny*
Nurul Haq x Ebadullah	,,
Khoorshid Meah x Mossoudali	,,
Abdul Jabbar x Hamid Ali	,,
Syed Ahmad x Ruckbatali	*Lascar*
Sikander Badsha x Mohabbatali	,,
Yazul Moolook x Abdool Allee	,,
Jabal Hawk x Abdool Mozid	,,
Salamatullah x Abbass Ali	,,
Abdul Barrick x Abdul Aziz	,,
Akel Ali x Asmat Ali	,,
Hazibar Rahman x Omer Ali	,,
Mujibul Haque x Abdul Karim	,,
Wali Mian x Raqbat Ali	,,
Ali Ahmad x Anwar Ali	,,
Matiur Rahman x Hamid	,,
Mozid Mian x Abdul Jubbar	,,
Mohamad Haroon x Mohamad Meah	,,
Murshid Mian x Abdul Barie	*Bhandary*
Kishori x Baboo Lall	*Topass*
Mungal x Sokhi	,,
Kholill Rahman x Dewan Ali	*F. Serang*
Nozib Ahamode x Mosad Allee	*First Tindal*
Abdool Azis x Eusuph Allee	*Second Tindal*
Syed Rahman x Keramat Ali	*Cassab*
Mohamd. Islam x Abdul Majid	*Lampman*
Fozore Ali x Hamdoo Mian	*Donkeyman*
Soozat Allee x Korone Alle	*Oilman*

Abdul Karim x Borhanuddin	*Oilman*
Jalal Ahmad x Asmut Ali	,,
Fazal Karim x Asmat Ali	*Fireman*
Molakat Joma x Anwor Ali	,,
Doola Mian x Eusuph Ali	,,
Abdul Hakim x Asmath Ali	,,
Abdul Suttar x Abdul Ghafur	,,
Muni Ahmad x Abdul Majid	,,
Nur Ahmad x Abdur Rashid	,,
Belait Ali x Fazal Rahman	,,
Ali Ahmad x Thanda Mian	,,
Amin Rahman x Abdool Meah	*Coal Trimmer*
Raja Meah x Anoo Meah	,,
Tufail Ahmad x Hasmat Ali	,,
Abdul Latif x Ahsanulla	,,
Abdul Karim x Abdus Subhan	,,
Sherazul Hawk x Ahamode Ali	,,
Abdul Rashid x Mohamd. Latoo	,,
Nesar Ahmad x Chunoo Meah	,,
Maqsul Hosain x Sadaw Ali	,,
Abdul Ghafur x Musharraf Ali	,,
Mohamed x Mohorom	,,
A. R. Pais x M. B. Pais	*Butler*
C. Rodrigues x J. Rodrigues	*Chief Cook and Baker*
P. Cardoze x S. Cardoze	*Second Cook*
L. Caldeird x H. Caldeird	*Fourth Cook*
E. C. Rodrigues x M. Rodrigues	*Pantryman*
F. DeCosta x J. M. DeCosta	*Captain's Boy*
Sk. Kinoo x Lall Chand	*Chief Engineer's Boy*
T. Rodrigues x F. E. Rodrigues	*General Servant Boy*
J. A. DeCosta x R. DeCosta	,,
J. P. Collasco x L. V. Collasco	,,
T. M. Fernandes x Augustine Fernandes	,,
J. M. Costa x F. Costa	*Half General Servant Boy*
Jetoo x Ruckber	*Topass*

s.s. *GANDARA*

Abdul Ghafur x Abdur Kader	*Seacunny*
Rustom Ali x Abdul Kader Munshi	*Lascar*
Salamatulla x Foizuddin	*Lascar*
Kishorilal x Chotey	*Topass*
Abdul Rahman x Johuroody	*Bhandary*
Mohamed Idris x Abdul	*Lampman*

Abdul Huq x Rahimulla	*Fireman*
Frances Xarir x G. F. Fernandes	*Chief Engineer's Boy*

s.s. *GARMULA*

Mulkay Joma x Muckbool Ali	*Tindal*
Parsy Mian x Abdul Karim	*Seacunny*
Maqbul Ahmad x Ramzan Ali	,,
Mozafar Ali x Mohd. Hanif	*Lascar*
Mustafa Rahman x Amin Shariff	,,
Abdul Monan x Abdul Mozid	*First Tindal*
Abdul Mojid x Hamid Ali	*Oilman*
Abdul Jabbar x Meajan	*Fireman*
Keramat Ali x Hamdoo Meah	,,
Nozoo Mian x Abdul Karim	,,
Ashraf Ali x Abdul Soban	*Coal Trimmer*
Badsha Mian x Fozoo Mian	,,
Hasmat x Din Mohammad	*Bhandary*
Francis Almeida x Hose Almeida	*Pantryman*

s.s. *GOGRA*

Aminoody x Amjad Meah	*Engine Serang*
Rustom Ali x Nozim	*First Tindal*
Muslim x Wazuddin	*Second Tindal*
Ahmad Mian x Fazluddin	*Oilman*
Mumtaz Meah x Afiloody	,,
Salamatulla x Yeassin	,,
Hasmatulla x Hassan Ali	*Lampman*
Aslam Meah x Olly Meah	*Fireman*
Nazir Mian x Shamsheruddin	,,
Enoos Meah x Asgar Ali	,,
Athar Meah x Ossimuddin	,,
Ahamadullah x Salamatullah	,,
Akhtaruzzaman x Abid Mian	,,
Ismail x Abdool Hakim	,,
Abdul Salam x Mohd. Ishaque	,,
Nazir Mian x Attore Allee	,,
Monir Ahmad x Serazul Haque	,,
Akhtarzzaman x Muslim	*Coal Trimmer*
Rashid Mian x Islam Miah	,, ,,
Nazir Meah x Ismail	,, ,,
Wali Meah x Noor Meah	,, ,,
Habibullah x Ibrahim	,, ,,

Salamatullah x Henza Gazi	*Coal Trimmer*
Mobarakullah x Sona Meah	" "
Sherazul Huq x Asad Meah	" "
Tobarak Ali x Fazar Ali	" "
Farzan Allee x Samad Allee	*Bhandary*
Hyder Allee x Wasuloodin	*Cassab*
Monir Ahmad x Roshan Ali	*Coal Trimmer*
Phagua x Balka	*Deck Topass*
Nathia Ghorai x Bino Ghorai	" "

s.s. *HATIMURA*

Nazir Ahmad x Mazore Ali	*Coal Trimmer*
Azizore Rahman x Anwar Ali	*1st Engineer Tindal*
J. A. Ferras x P. Ferras	*General Servant Boy*

s.s. *INDORA*

Syed Ali x Asghar Ali	*Seacunny*
M. Pereira x L. Pereira	*Chief Engr.'s Boy*

s.s. *KHEDIVE ISMAIL*

Antonia Pinto	*Butler*
Joseph P. Miranda	*Chief Cook*
Louis Fernandes	*Second Cook*
Sebastiao M. Rodrigues	" "
Jose Sebastiao Furtado	*Asst. V/Cook*
Baptisto Gama	" "
Simon D'Souza	*Asst. Baker*
Ladros D'Souza	*Baker's Mate*
Pascol D'Souza	*Butcher*
Vincent Mathias	*Butcher's Mate*
Minguel Fernandes	*1st Class Pantryman*
Domingo M. Dias	*2nd Class Pantryman*
Bernard D'Souza	*Pantrymate*
Simon Furtado	"
Caitan F. Vaz	*General Servant*
Alfonso Britto	*Chief Engineer's Boy*
Valentin Pereira	*General Servant*
Floriano Marquis	"
Manuel Fernandes	"
John D'Souza	"
Louis Crasto	"
Thomas Menezies	"

John D'Souza	*Captain's Boy*
Antonio M. D'Costa	*General Servant*
Joao C. Azavedo	,,
Abel M. Alfonso	,,
Menine Gomes	,,
Barnardo Fernandes	,,
Antonia S. Ferrao	,,
Joaquim P. Fernandes	,,
Pascoal Pinto	,,
Felix Pereira	,,
Pascoal Correa	,,
Robert Pinto	,,
Ignacio Fernandes	,,
Gaberial D'Souza	,,
Raphael Oliveira	,,
Jerom D'Soûza	,,
Roque F. Fernandes	,,
Ellias Taero	,,
Pelegirino Rodrigues	,,
Augustino Martins	,,
Domingo F. Gomes	,,
Custodio Fernandes	*Iceman*
John Monteiro	,,
Ladru Laslado	*Scullion*
Salvadore Dias	*Topass*
Victorino DeCosta	,,
Gonsalinho Marrel	,,
Pedro M. Furtado	,,
Anthoney Rocha	,,
Salvadore Gonsalves	*Asst. V/Cook*
Casmir D'Souza	,, *Mate*
Sabastiao Fernandes	*Troop Chief Cook*
Ramad Gama	*Troop Second Cook*
Lawrence Pinto	,, ,,
Remedio Rodrigues	*Troop Asst. V/Cook*
Alexio P. Pereira	*Troop Asst. Baker*
Douglas R. Fernandes	,, ,,
Louis Sanchia	,, ,, *Mate*
Jose S. Berreto	*Troop Butcher*
Joaquin M. Dias	*Troop Asst. Butcher*
Caetan Pires	*Troop Butcher's Mate*
Antonio J. Monteiro	*Troop Storekeeper's Mate*
Cruz F. P. D'Sa	*Cant. Storekeeper's Mate*

Antony Antao	*General Servant*
Presentaco C. Veigas	*Storekeeper*
A. J. I. Gomes	*Baker*
Antonio Lobo	*Storekeeper's Mate*
Abdul Qader Thanda Meah	*Lascar*
Sookoor x Hasmoo	*Fireman Bhandary*
Abdul Ali Mubarak Ali	*Coal Trimmer*
Belayat Ali Goolam Ali	*Lascar*

s.s. *MADURA*

Abu Taher x Zamiruddin	*Deck Bhandary Mate*
Durbash Allee x Attore Alee	*Iceman*
Motia Rahman x Safar Ali	*Coal Trimmer*

s.s. *MALDA*

Pednoo Fernandes	*Second Cook*

s.s. *MUNDRA*

Omed x Peeroo	*Serang*
Hatim x Alibar Sk.	*Tindal*
Latiff x Afazal	*Cassab*
Abdur Rahim x Hakim Ali	*Winchman*
Faiz Ahmed x Md. Ali	*Seacunny*
Noor Ahmad	,,
Tobaruck Hossein x Wazzer Sk.	*Lascar*
Dewan Ali x Kala Meah Depari	,,
Samiruddin Santoo Sk.	,,
Abdul Aziz x Aslam	,,
Mir Hikmatali x Mir Dorbesh Ali	,,
Mohim Sk. x Nehal Sk.	,,
Aminal Huq x Abdul Qadir	,,
Amin Sharif x Ashraf Ali	,,
Pear Ahmed x Akrome Ali	,,
Abrar Hossain x Nassir	*Bhandary*
Madhu x Phelo	*Topass*
Abdul Ghani x Mohd. Wali	*Engine Room 1st Tindal*
Taher Ali x Modaris Ali	*Iceman*
Nurul Huq x Lall Mian	*Oilman*
Sheraz Hawk x Anwar Ali	,,
Habibullah x Enoosullah	*Fireman*
Secunder Allee x Munsoor Ali	,,
Shamsul Huq x Avock Ali	,,

Osman Ali x Aslam	*Fireman*
Habiz Ali x Saberali	,,
Keramat Ali x Abdul Mozid	,,
Nazir Ahmed x Muslim	,,
Ansur Ali x Jitoo Mian	*Coal Trimmer*
Nurul Huq x Muslim	,, ,,
Mokone Ali x Emrath Ali	,, ,,
Ebrahim x Safar Ali	,, ,,
Ashrufali x Sk. Qurban	*Second Cook*
Sk. Khalill x Salimuddin	*Fourth Cook*
Shamsuddin Chowdhury x Makoo Chowdhury	*Capt.'s Boy*
Sunoo x Abdul Ghany	*General Servant Boy*
Ayaz Ali x Abdul Basher	,,
I. C. Dias x A. Dias	*Half General Servant*
Abbas Ali x Sk. Ghany	,,
Dunghai Naik x Aparti Naik	*Topass*
Rogue Rodrigues x J. X. Rodrigues	*Chief Engineer's Boy*
Mohanlal Agrawal	*Surgeon*
Ratnaswami	*General Servant Boy*

Passenger Crew for Harrison Line proceeded by the s.s. *MUNDRA*

Mohd. Yeasin x Sk. Ismail	*1st Tindal*
Mowla Bux x Habu	*Cassab*
Cochee x Eunus	*Lascar*
Abdul Rashid x Ansoor Ali	,,
Moorshid Meah x Sadock Allee	,,
Habeeoolla x Abdul Rahman	,,
Sk. Mickbool x Sk. Meyboob	,,
Sultan Ahmad x Abdul Majid	,,
Medhi Husan x Chuni	,,
Baboo Lall x Chamari	*Topass*
Abdulla x Mohiuddin	*Bhandary*
Calcuttee x Jiten	*Lascar and Topass*
Ismail x Qasim Ali	*Cassab*
Afazullah x Narullah	*Greaser*
Mushruffullah x Sadir Mohd.	*Fireman*
Ismail x Abdul	,,
Suruj Mian x Kashir Mohomad	,,
Mofizolla x Hamidoolla	,,
Suraz Mian x Babroo Mian	,,
Marfat Khan x Dowlat Khan	,,

Jahir Mian x Ayatulla	*Fireman*
Hatimoolla x Sooltan Mohd.	,,
Arfanulla x Sefathulla	,,
Ijjutulla x Omerulla	,,
Mobarkullah x Abdulla	*Coal Trimmer*
Karmat Ali x Collimulla	,, ,,
Abdul Halim x Asanulla	,, ,,
Johidullah x Jobanullah	,, ,,
Mossadar Ali x Dnone Meah	,, ,,
Umberoolla x Foorcanoolla	*Bhandary*
Sk. Dholoo x Sk. Fazil	*Second Cook*
Mohorum x Johoroody	*Officer's Boy*
Mohd. Ismail x Sk. Mosab	*Messroom Boy*
Mojibur Rahman x Rahmat Ali	*Saloon Boy*
Sk. Basu x Sk. Fazil	*Scullion*

Passenger Crew for Asiatic Line proceeded by the s.s. *MUNDRA*

Naderuzzaman Ismatali	*Seacunny*
Siddick Ahmad x Lall Mohd.	,,
Golam Hossain x Ekbal Hossain	*Lascar*
Khursid Allum x Fazal Rahaman	,,
Abu Sukur x Ismatali	,,
Abdul Hossain x Ranzanali	,,
Mendijan x Alimooddin	*Bhandary*
Kobad Miah x Abdul Currim	*Greaser*
Abdul Huq x Anwarali	,,
Ghulam Rahaman x Aslam	*Fireman*
Muslim x Abdool Majid	,,
Abdul Aziz x Jeanuddin	,,
Mofizuddin x Haji Hamidulla	*Coal Trimmer*
Mohd. Yeacoob x Sk. Budhoo	*Butler*
Sk. Shazada x Sk. Rajamiah	*General Servant Boy*

s.s. *NARDANA*

Abbas Ali x Kobeer	*Winchman*
Shabul Hamid x Harunur Rashid	*Seacunny*
Abdul Jalil x Corban Ali	,,
Abdul Goffor x Ameer Ali	*Lascar*
Abdul Hai x Baddaruddin	,,
Said Ahmad x Faizullah	,,
Ali Hossein Naboo x Naboo	*Barber*
Nozoo Mian x Abdul Karim	*Donkeyman*

Nossore Ahmad x Neamat Ali	*Oilman*
Abdul Barrick x Razack Ali	,,
Abdul Karim x Toofan Ali	*Fireman*
Monoo Meah x Bosiroolla	,,
Abdul Jolill x Keramut Ali	,,
Matiur Rahman x Seedique Ahmad	,,
Abdul Mian x Sadear Ali	*Coal Trimmer*
Mobarack Ali x Abdul	,, ,,

s.s. *NEURALIA*

Gonoo Mian	*Coal Trimmer*
Abdool Majid	*General Servant Boy*

s.s. *NIRPURA*

Mithan Bansi	*Deck Topass*
Ignacio Cardozo	*Captain's Boy*
Ignacio Caetan Fernandes	*General Servant*

Passenger Crew for s.s. *Orna* proceeded by the s.s. *REHMANI*

Nagar Vishram	*Lascar*
Luckman Bhicka	,,
John David Pinto	*General Servant*

s.s. *QUILOA*

Janoo x Jitoo	*Topass*
F. Baptista x M. Baptista	*Fourth Cook*
Gunuai x Bauria	*Topass*

s.s. *ROHNA*

Muklesur Rahman x Umberali	*F. Serang*
Abdool Mozid x Hari Bepari	*First Tindal*
Gonoo Meah x Abassallee	*Second Tindal*
Eman Allee x Rajab Allee	*Donkeyman*
Abdul Latif x Chand Mian	*Lampman*
Habib Rahman x Tozoomeah	*Iceman*
Fozoo Meah x Bachoo Mohd.	*Oilman*
Noor Bux x Abdul Meah	,,
Mohamed Meah x Mathy Meah	,,
Azizor Rohoman x Jamid Allee	,,
Afzal x Eman Ali	*Fireman*
Nehazur Rahman x Meherali	,,

Sharazul Huq x Hasan Ali	*Fireman*
Altoo Meah x Amir Ali	*Coal Trimmer*
Muslim Meah x Islam Meah	,, ,,
Muruzali x Wazidali	,, ,,
Jewa Ranchord	*First Tindal*
Muckan Chibba	*Cassab*
Doolab Seeba	*Seacunny*
Makan Lalla	,,
Goven Vallab	,,
Vallubb Rama	*Lascar*
Meetha Fackeer	,,
Fackeer Sooka	,,
Valub Ranchord	,,
Fackeer Meetha	,,
Manchia Dettia	,,
Bhana Kalidas	,,
Lalla Karia	,,
Naroon Jadhow	,,
Nathoo Gandha	,,
Daya Kallia	,,
Daira Deiva	,,
Mohamed x Dar Bukoh	,,
Shandar Seeba	,,
Purbhoo Lalloo	,,
Karia Goven	,,
Mahadeo Kallia	,,
Bawa Veera	,,
Lalloo Karia	,,
Ranchord Daya	*Half Lascar*
Surta Bihari	*Topass*
Sangar Chowara	,,
F. Gomes	*Storekeeper*
Francis Pereira	*Headwaiter*
Vincent Lobo A. Lobo	*Second Cook*
Martin Fernandes	*Pantryman's Mate*
Janowal Fernandes	*Baker*
Louis Pinto x Anton Pinto	*Assistant Baker*
Justiciano Coelho	*Butcher*
Marian P. Coorea	*Butcher's Mate*
Basil Rodriques	*First Pantryman*
Mariano Lopes	*Second Pantryman*
Santan Fernandes	*Pantryman's Mate*
C. S. Fernandes	*Chief Engineer's Boy*

Jerominio N. Pais	*General Servant*
Mathews C. Gomes	,,
Caetan Francis Fernandes	,,
Gasper Piedade Fernandes	,,
Francis Fernandes	,,
Sabastiao Piedade	,,
Roque B. Fernandes	,,
Joaquim Rozario Godinho	,,
Roque Pereira	,,
John D'Souza	,,
Ignacio Francis Menezies	,,
Thomas Fernandes x Antonio Manoel	,,
J. M. Fernandes	,,
S. P. A. Paes	,,
Francis Fernandes	*Scullion*
Nicolan Fernandes	,,
Joaquim V. Alfonso	*Topass*
Ignacio Fernandes	,,
Alex D'Costa	*Troop Butler*
R. C. Almeida	*Troop Storekeeper*
J. D. Cardoso	*Canteen Steward*
C. D'Silva	*Troop Assistant/Canteen Steward*
Jose Fernandes	*Troop Chief Cook*
Jerome Fernandes	*Troop Second Cook*
Laurence Fernandes	,, ,,
Caetan Collaco	*Troop Third Cook*
Ozario Caetan Fernandes	*Troop Baker*
Francisco Dias	*Troop Assistant Baker*
Joaquim R. Godinho	*Troop Baker's Mate*
Bendoo Correa	*Troop Butcher*
Octaviano D. M. Pinto	*Troop Assistant Butcher*
Verodian Fernandes	*Troop Butcher's Mate*
Natividade Fegueredo	*Troop General Servant*
Jose Domingos Fernandes	,,
Augustino Fernandes	,,
S. Fernandes	,,
F. Cardina	,,
Phillip Fernandes	*General Servant*
Gregory Tauro	,,
M. F. Cabral	,,
Manuel Jose Pereira	*Fourth Cook*
Sebastiao Fernandes	,, ,,

Joao Jose Timoti	*Scullion*
Santan Monterio	*Topass*
D. Baretto	*Half General Servant*
Anthon Baretto	*Troop Third Cook*
Jose Minguel Furtado	*Troop Baker's Mate*
Alexander Leitao	*Troop Scullion*
M. Antao	*General Servant*
R. Sequeira	*Topass*
A. D'Costa	*General Servant*
C. P. Vaz	,,

s.s. *SIR HARVEY ADAMSON*

Jan Mahomed	*Purser*
Fong Sing	*Chinese Carpenter*
Yeacub Ali	*Serang*
Yeacub Ali	*Tindal*
Muckbul Ahamed	*Cassab*
Abdul Razaque	*Winchman*
Shariatoolla	*Seacunny*
Seedique Ahmed	,,
Allee	,,
Abdul Jalill	*Lascar*
Habibullah	,,
Leakat Ali	,,
Serajuddin	,,
Faizullah	,,
Syed Ali	,,
Mohamed Azim	,,
Fazal Ahmed	,,
Omer Meah	,,
Abdul Mannan	,,
Syed Rahman	*Bhandary*
Ramcharitra	*Topass*
Chella Duria	,,
Ibrahim	*Barber*
Fazal Rahman	*Serang*
Darbesh Ali	*First Tindal*
Abdul Malik	*Second Tindal*
Abdul Samad	*Cassab*
Currim Bux	*Lampman*
Nazir Ahamed	*Oilman*
Saleh Ahamed	,,

Badsha Meah	*Fireman*
Abdul Kahleq	,,
Abdul Rashid	,,
Badsha Mian	*Coal Trimmer*
Doola Mian	,, ,,
Cherag Ali	,, ,,
Monir Ahamed	*Bhandary*
Abdul Mazid	*Fireman*
Ersad Ali	,,
Noor Islam	,,
Mohd. Yeacub	*Butler*
Kala Achha	*Chief Cook*
Abdul Rahman	*Second Cook*
John Sing	*Third Cook*
Lall Meah	*Pantryman*
Sk. Minno	*Captain's Boy*
Abdul Ghaffur	*Chief Engineer's Boy*
Johoor	*General Servant*
Sk. Abdul Khaliq	,,
Fazla Rahman	,,
A. Swami	,,
Iyya Swami Fernando	,,
Abdul Aziz	,,
Gazi	*Topass*
Budhia	,,

s.s. *TALAMBA*

John F. Fernandes	*Butler*
Jose Gomes	*Half General Servant*
Sumya Bijla	*Lascar*
Pheroo Kersingh	*Topass*

s.s. *TILAWA*

A. Britto	*General Servant*
Eplifant Fernandes	,,
Af Saruddin Allimuddin	,,
A. X. Fernandes	*Scullion*
Chanda Mamjee	*Hindu Cook*
Bhawanji Manji	,, ,,
Hussein Sirkhod	*Mahomedan Cook*
Umer Hossein	,, ,,

Sonali Khodad Morad	*Laundry Manager*
Equbal Ghulam Hyder	*Laundryman*
Abdur Rashid Chonoo Mian	*Lascar*
Secunder Meah Umtore Ali	*Fireman*
Abdul Sattar Bashád Ali	*Coal Trimmer*
Hafizor K. Dhaman	,, ,,
Feroze Ali Hazoo	,, ,,
Abdul Samad x Abdul Mataleb	*Fireman*
Sultan Ahmad x Yeacoob Ali	*Coal Trimmer*
Sona Mea x Badur Rahman	,, ,,
Farock Ahmed	*Cassab*

Passenger Crew for s.s. *Takliwa* proceeded by the s.s. *TILAWA*

C. A. Paes	*Butler*
J. Desa	*Butcher*
Domingo J. M. Gama	*Captain's Boy*
Santaritto Fernandes	*Chief Engineer's Boy*
Diogo Maria Vaz	*General Servant*
Rozahino Almeida	,,
J. Vaz	,,
Daniel Collaco	,,
Francis Xavier Texeira	,,
Xavier Louis	,,
Ignacio Manoel Pais	,,
Bernard Fernandes	*Topass*
Salvadore Fernandes	*Troop Fourth Cook*
J. D'Silva	*Troop G.S.*
Pema Muckan	*Lascar*
Bhartu Dhuli	*Topass*
Ghisoo Jiya	,,
Jagnam Gangadial	,,

s.s. *WARFIELD*

Ahmed Mohamed Jaffer	*Coal Trimmer*
Ram Bhaya	*Deck Serang*
Narayan Jeewa	*Cassab*
Lackman Nathoo	*Tindal*
Jeewa Panchia	*Winchman*
Naran Veerjee	*Seacunny*
Ditta Valla	,,
Bhim Bawal	,,
Valla Jeewa	*Lascar*

Lalla Nathoo	*Lascar*
Panchia Munjee	,,
Chania Boodhia	,,
Heera Nathoo	,,
Ditta Jagu	,,
Jogu Naron	,,
Kessa Valla	,,
Rama Haree	,,
Dewa Bhim	,,
Lalla Heera	,,
Haria Banji	*Bhandary*
Armogan Veera	*Topass*
Rama Jeewa	*Lascar*
Kika Doya	,,
Keshwa Hognath	*Topass*
Martin Fernandes	*Butler*
Augustin D'Souza	*Ship's Cook and Baker*
Avertano Fernandes	*Second Cook*
Domingos Fernandes	*Fourth Cook*
R. F. Rodrigues	*Pantryman*
S. Pereira	*Captain's Boy*
L. Pereira	*Chief Engineer's Boy*
Minino Fernandes	*General Servant*
Francis Fernandes	,,
Roque Clemant	,,
Jose P. Deniz	,,
Rozario M. Rodrigues	*Half General Servant*
Rozario Fernandes	*Topass*

s.s. *WAROONGA*

Silvester Fernandes	*Butcher*
P. Cardoso	*Captain's Boy*
C. Fernandes	*General Servant*
S. Carvalho	,,
S. Fernandes	*Half General Servant*
Santan Fernandes	*Topass*

s.s. *WINKFIELD*

Kanu Luckman	*Lascar*
Octaviana D'Costa	*General Servant*

2

PRISONERS-OF-WAR

It's a warm wind, the west wind, full of birds' cries;
I never hear the west wind but tears are in my eyes.
For it comes from the west lands, the old brown hills,
And April's in the west wind, and daffodils.

The West Wind—JOHN MASEFIELD

O.H.M.S.

Lt. K. R. Alger, R.N.R.
Lt. Comdr. A. G. Brooks, D.S.C., R.N.R.

s.s. *CHILKA*

A. R. Andrew	*Chief Officer*	
K. M. Feast	*Second Officer*	(died in captivity)
G. B. Hodges	*Third Officer*	,, ,,
J. B. Kerr	*Fourth Engineer*	,, ,,
G. S. M. Davidson	*Junior Engineer*	
K. S. Shahabuddin, B.E.M.	*Cadet*	

s.s. *DEVON*

R. Redwood	*Commander*
S. Henderson	*Chief Officer*
F. C. Conolly	*Second Officer*
W. Pritchard	*Third Officer*
R. S. Beesley	*Fourth Officer*
A. G. Dowdney	*Cadet*
N. G. Brodie	*Cadet*

W. Errington	*Cadet*
H. W. Hughes	*Cadet*
D. N. Scott	*Cadet*
R. H. Bartley	*Purser*
J. Henderson	*Chief Engineer*
J. W. Douthwaite	*Second Engineer Officer*
K. C. MacDougall	*Third Engineer Officer*
J. Andrew	*Fourth Engineer Officer*
J. P. Cullis	*Junior Engineer Officer*
J. C. Davis	*Junior Engineer Officer*
F. Rouse	*Junior Engineer Officer*
G. Ratchford	*Junior Engineer*
R. Smith	*Junior Engineer*
P. K. Rea	*Chief Ref. Officer*
A. Miller	*2 Ref. Engineer Officer*
A. H. Hallen	*Surgeon*
H. W. Ferguson	*Carpenter*

M.S. *DUMRA*

H. T. Graham — *Chief Officer* (died in captivity)

S.S. *MADURA*

E. W. Crocker — *Chief Steward*

S.S. *MATA HARI*—(P.& O. vessel—under full charter to Admiralty —H.M.S.)

Temp. Lieut. A. C. Carston, R.N.R.	*Commander*
Temp. sub. Lieut. A. H. Hogge, R.N.R.	*Chief Officer*
Temp. Lieut. (E) F. J. Lumley, R.N.R.	*Chief Engineer*
Temp. sub. Lieut. (E) H. M. MacGregor, R.N.R.	*Second Engineer*
Temp. sub. Lieut. (E) T. R. Gordon, R.N.R.	*Third Engineer*
Temp. Actg. sub. Lieut. (E) W. McCrorie, R.N.R.	*Fourth Engineer*

S.S. *NOWSHERA*

J. N. Collins	*Commander*
D. E. Crowther	*Captain*
J. B. Cooke	*Chief Officer*
A. B. Stephens	*Second Officer*

L. Chisholm	*Third Officer*
F. A. Cahill	*R.N.*
H. Simpson	*Cadet*
A. M. Hatton	*Cadet*
C. Higgins	*Chief Engineer Officer*
R. A. Philp	*Second Engineer*
W. E. Garrod	*Third Engineer*
J. G. Kendall	*Fourth Engineer Officer*
T. Dixon	*Junior Engineer Officer*
J. Harrison	*Junior Engineer Officer*
J. H. L. Pasco	*Junior Engineer Officer*
J. I. Jones	*Gunner*
R. C. Bellew	*Junior Engineer Officer*

INDIAN SEAMEN

s.s. *DEVON*

Abid Ali	*Lascar*
Badsham Mian	*Lascar*
Manuar Mllee	*Donkeyman*
Ali Ahmad	*Winchman*
Ayed Ahmed	*Seacunny*
Lukni Naik	*Deck Topass*
Elahi Bux	*Lascar*
Magbul Ahmode	*Seacunny*
Zabed Ali	*Fireman*
Sona Mia	,,
Jantar Ali	*Coal Trimmer*
Mcfizuddin	*Lascar*
Amir Ali	*Fireman*
Foorcan Ali	,,
Haris Ali	*Coal Trimmer*
Ardjudales	*Lascar*
Mahboob Abdul	,,
Nazir Ali	,,
Bhagan x Saipoo	*E.R. Bhandary*

s.s. *GOALPARA*

S. Fernandes	*Pantryman*
S. Ferrao	*Chief Engineer's Boy*
S. d'Souza	*Galley Servant*

S. Rodriques	*Galley Servant*
J. F. Pinto	*Captain's Boy*
J. P. Pullenayagam	*Galley Servant*
Salem	*Deck Bhandary*
A. Samhod	*Barber*
Sallihamod	*Selwale*
Gonumiah	*Fireman*
A. Zellil	,,
Kallamiah	,,
Abdulkader	*Coal Trimmer*
Kallamiah	,, ,,
Abdulajiz	,, ,,
F. J. Martins	*Butler*

s.s. *NOWSHERA*

Dr. Mrityunjoy Mitra	*Doctor*
Bahauddin Rashid	*Butler*
Mustapha	*Deck Bhandary*
Sheriat Uha	*Serang*
Abdur Rahman	*General Servant Boy*
Basir Ulla	*Deck Cassab*
Abdul Rashid	*Fireman*
Secundar Ali	,,
Arab Ali	*Coal Trimmer*
Anoo Meah	*Seacunny*
Lalloo x Koyrati	*Deck Topass*
Abdul Latif	*Lascar*
Abdul Aziz	*Fireman*
Arab Ali	*Trimmer*

ADDENDUM

KNIGHTHOOD

SIR ERNEST GEOFFREY BROOKES, R.N.R.
(*Commodore, British India Fleet*)

3

HONOURS AND AWARDS

Yet though their splendour may have ceased to be,
Each played her sovereign part in making me;
Now I return my thanks with heart and lips,
For the great queenliness of all those ships.

Ships—JOHN MASEFIELD

DISTINGUISHED SERVICE ORDER, DISTINGUISHED SERVICE CROSS and BAR to DISTINGUISHED SERVICE ORDER

LT. COMMANDER J. I. MILLER, R.N.R. (*Chief Officer*)

For outstanding gallantry, fortitude and resolution during the Battle of Crete.

For gallantry and distinguished services in the withdrawal from the Beaches of Greece under fire and in face of many difficulties of many thousands of troops of the Allied Armies.

DISTINGUISHED SERVICE CROSS

LT. COMMANDER C. L. BROADHURST, R.N.R. (*Chief Officer*)
LT. COMMANDER G. F. PARKER, R.D., R.N.R. (*Chief Officer*)

For outstanding courage, leadership, resource and determination during the assault on Anzio and in subsequent bombardments in support of the Army and in maintaining an unbroken flow of supplies which accomplished the building up' of the beach-head despite bombing, mining and bombardment by shore batteries.

LT. COMMANDER A. G. BROOKS, R.N.R. (*Chief Officer*)

For bravery in action and under fire at Tobruk.

LT. COMMANDER W. R. K. CLARK, R.N.R.
For bravery, endurance and devotion to duty in North African waters.

CAPTAIN F. L. SAMPSON
For gallantry and distinguished services in the withdrawal from the Beaches of Greece under fire and in face of many and great difficulties of many thousands of troops of the Allied Armies.

BENJAMIN ANDREW ROGERS (*Chief Officer*), R.N.
LT. DENNIS BUNN, R.N., R.N.R. (*Third Officer*)
R. A. SPIERS (*Second Officer*)
For gallantry and devotion to duty while serving in Greek Waters.

K. J. BABER, R.I.N.R. (*Cadet Lt.*)
For courage, enterprise and leadership in Light Coastal Forces of the Royal Indian Navy in hazardous operations.

LT. J. M. STEADMAN, R.N.R. (*Cadet*)
For outstanding courage and skill and devotion to duty in successful patrols in one of H.M. Submarines.

A. MACINTOSH (*Chief Engineer Officer*)
For courage, skill and devotion to duty in operations off the Indian coast.

GEORGE MEDAL

LT. D. W. SPEIRS, R.N.R. (*Second Officer*)
For gallantry and undaunted devotion to duty.

COMMANDER OF THE BRITISH EMPIRE

J. B. HENDERSON (*General Manager, Garden Reach Workshops*)
J. WALLACE (*Chief Engineer Officer*)

ORDER OF THE BRITISH EMPIRE

CAPTAIN J. L. BEATTY
CAPTAIN W. BIRD
When the ship was sunk by gun-fire from a Japanese submarine, the master saw the ship's boat away and then embarked in a boat which he navigated to the Dutch East Indies. He saw his ship's company housed and the wounded attended to. Then, with six volunteers, he set out in a ship's lifeboat for Ceylon. On the twenty-fourth day of the passage he was rescued by a Greek vessel being then off Madras.

Appendices

Captain R. H. A. Bond
Captain F. Caffyn
Captain A. D. Davies

The ship was torpedoed at night. She listed so sharply that the Master gave orders to abandon her. Four boats got away without incident but one in charge of the Master struck the sea stern first. The plug was knocked out, some equipment was lost and the boat began to fill. During this time, the enemy began to shell the sinking ship.

The Master had the boat baled out, transferred some men from another lifeboat which was even more damaged, and set sail for land. The rudder had been lost and steering was done by oar. The Master sailed his deeply laden craft 500 miles to safety. For eight days he maintained steady discipline and by his good seamanship saved the lives of the twenty-six men under his care.

Captain T. E. C. Earl

The ship, sailing alone, was torpedoed. Extensive damage was caused and, as she was sinking, abandonment was ordered. Although one of the boats was up-ended in the heavy weather, the crew got away successfully in the remaining boats and all eventually reached safety without the loss of a single life.

After ensuring that all those on board were got away, the Master took charge of one of the boats. The voyage was arduous but although many of the occupants were suffering from exposure and exhaustion all were brought to safety. The boat was within one day's sail of port when, after sixteen days, it was picked up. Captain Earl displayed great courage and skill throughout and it was due to his excellent organisation that all persons on board were able to abandon ship without casualty.

Seacunny Ellie Bux x Zafir Ali was of great assistance to the Master during the boat voyage, his courage and cheerfulness setting a fine example to the others in the boat.

The Chief Officer was in charge of the second boat and showed courage and leadership of a high order. The boat made a voyage of fourteen days and was navigated by Mr. Hopkins, unaided, to port. It was entirely due to his skill and leadership that the occupants reached safety.

The Second Officer took charge of the third boat. After a varied and adventurous voyage which lasted ten days a landfall was made. The landing place, however, was uninhabited and Mr. Brookfield, provisioning his party with stores and gear from the boat, marched them for three days across the desert to a small habitation where he was able to get another boat in which they made a voyage of five days to a nearby port.

CAPTAIN A. A. LEWIS

The ship made several voyages to Tobruk. She was attacked by dive-bombers and badly damaged. The Master has shown courage and fine judgment in his handling of the vessel.

CAPTAIN J. W. MILNE

The ship made three voyages to Greece. During her first voyage she was subjected to a high-level bombing attack, and on the second and third to dive-bombing attacks, once by no less than twenty-five machines. The Master's superb seamanship saved his command from destruction. Without the aid of charts, in darkness, he navigated her successfully up the narrow channel of the Euripus to Chalkis where a strong tide runs.

CAPTAIN W. SINCLAIR

CAPTAIN C. C. TAYLOR

The ship was torpedoed in darkness and sustained severe damage. The engines were restarted and for thirty hours she was not only kept afloat and under way, but maintained her position in convoy. The weather got worse, however, and, with the engine-room flooding and the ship sinking by the stern, abandonment was ordered.

Captain Taylor showed outstanding qualities of courage and leadership throughout and made a determined effort to save his ship. When this was found to be impossible it was due to his excellent organisation and efficiency that the ship was successfully abandoned.

CAPTAIN P. TAYLOR

N. HOUFTON (*Chief Officer*)

One of H.M. transports arrived at Berbera with troops and stores which were urgently required by our forces in British Somaliland. Mr. Houfton, by his fine example, leadership, and hard work, greatly helped the unloading which had to be done into lighters with the least possible delay. His services were invaluable.

JAMES MANSON (*Chief Engineer Officer*)

G. D. STEWART (*Chief Engineer Officer*)

COMMANDER (E) F. M. PASKINS, R.N.R. (*Chief Engineer Officer*)

A. A. WILSON (*General Manager, Mazagon Dock Ltd., Bombay*)

MEMBER OF THE BRITISH EMPIRE

R. H. AYRES (*Second Officer*)

The ship was torpedoed and three boats were got away. One in command of the Second Mate set out with thirty-one men in her, eight of them Europeans and twenty-three Indians. Only the Second Mate had any skill with boats.

It was a dark night and heavy seas were running so they lay-to a sea anchor until dawn when they set sail and steered East.

Mr. Ayres fixed the water ration at two dippers a day and gave the Indians who were least able to withstand the cold the forward part of the boat under the canvas cover, and all the blankets.

After seven days only seven remained alive, the rest having died of exposure or drinking sea water.

By the eighth day the water had gone and the men's hands and feet were badly frost-bitten. After thirteen days land was sighted. They were too weak to use the oars so they ran under shortened sail for the inhospitable shore. A comber broached them to overturn the boat and all hands were thrown into the sea. Another breaker righted her and the Second Mate pulled himself aboard and helped to drag in others. Again she turned turtle. The only three men to survive this last ordeal now clung to the keel. One let go his hold and the others were too weak to help him. The Second Mate and a seaman struck out desperately for shore. Helpers came and the seaman scrambled to a rock, but before he could be reached he was washed back into the sea and was not seen again.

Mr. Ayres was unconscious when hauled ashore. Undismayed by suffering and death he had kept a stout heart and done all a man could to comfort his shipmates and bring them to safety.

W. Brawn (*Chief Officer*)

M. G. Brookfield (*Second Officer*)
 See citation Captain Earl, O.B.E.

J. Beadle (*Second Engineer Officer*)

H. Cameron (*Chief Officer*)

D. J. Bardsley (*Chief Officer*)

E. Dinsdale (*Purser*)

T. G. Green (*Chief Officer*)

G. E. H. Hopkins (*Chief Officer*)
 See citation Captain Earl, O.B.E.

H. J. Lawton (*Second Engineer Officer*)

V. Rapson (*Chief Steward*)

BRITISH EMPIRE MEDAL

F. Huntley (*Q.M.*)

MENTIONED IN DESPATCHES

C. B. Mitchell (*Chief Officer*)

COMMENDED

Captain H. Goater
J. Smail (*Chief Officer*)
For brave conduct when they encountered enemy aircraft.

Captain N. Jamieson
For brave conduct when encountering enemy aircraft and submarines.

N. Apps (*Chief Officer*)
For brave conduct when encountering enemy aircraft.

H. C. Turner (*Chief Officer*)
For brave conduct when encountering enemy aircraft and submarines.

S. Button (deceased) (*Chief Engineer Officer*)
For brave conduct when encountering enemy submarines.

I. B. B. Robertson (*Chief Officer*)
For brave conduct when encountering enemy submarines.

E. G. Baines (*Chief Officer*)
For brave conduct when encountering enemy aircraft and submarines.

A. Ralph (*Second Officer*)
For brave conduct when encountering enemy aircraft.

G. M. Logie (*Cadet*)
For brave conduct when encountering enemy submarines.

A. C. Kirton (*Surgeon*)
For brave conduct when encountering enemy submarines.

G. Thomson (*Third Engineer*)
For brave conduct when encountering enemy submarines.

LLOYD'S WAR MEDAL

Captain W. Bird, O.B.E.
R. H. Ayres, M.B.E.

BRONZE STAR MEDAL (United States of America)

Captain T. H. Gill
In recognition of services to S.E.A.C.

CZECHO-SLOVAK MILITARY CROSS

Captain A. A. Kay
C. F. Du Sautoy (*Chief Officer*)
In recognition of their gallant conduct during the withdrawal of Czecho-Slovak troops from France in June 1940.

Appendices

ALBERT MEDAL

N. C. E. LITTLE (*Third Officer*)

In recognition of their services in rescuing four members of an aircraft of the R.A.F. Force in India which had made a forced landing. A boat had put off from the *Barpeta* to rescue the crew from the shore. The surf was very heavy and the boat was unable to pass through more than the first line of breakers about three-quarters of a mile off shore.

It was necessary for Mr. Little, Valla Pema and Jairam Narron to swim to the shore to assist the rescued men thro' the water to the boat. There was a strong and dangerous tide and a risk of being incapacitated by the men who were rescued, three of whom were unable to swim.

MEMBER OF THE BRITISH EMPIRE

MRITYUNJOY MITRA (*Ship's Doctor*)

When the ship was sunk by a raider, Dr. Mitra was taken prisoner and, after being kept in the prison ship for two and a half months, was interned in prisoners of war camps in France and Germany. While he was on board the prison ship, Dr. Mitra acted as doctor for the 349 prisoners. During his detention in Germany he attended Merchant Navy personnel, and in addition had 1,100 other prisoners under his care, mostly Orientals. Dr. Mitra showed exceptional devotion in undertaking this work voluntarily. There is little doubt that he did much to alleviate the sufferings of his fellow prisoners and to maintain general health in the camp, although his own health was so bad that it eventually resulted in his repatriation.

BRITISH EMPIRE MEDAL

K. S. SHAHABUDDIN (*Cadet*)

The ship was attacked by an enemy raider and so badly damaged by shellfire that abandonment was ordered. When the action commenced Cadet Shahabuddin manned the three-inch gun, but he was severely injured by an explosion when the ammunition locker was set on fire by a shell. In spite of his wounds he attempted to extinguish the fire with his bare hands and had to be forcibly removed to safety.

Throughout the five days he was in the lifeboat he bore intense pain without complaint, although the skin was burnt off his face and hands. He showed exceptional bravery, resolution and endurance and his devotion to duty was outstanding.

LALLA RUKMAN x RUKMON RAM (*Seacunny*)

For meritorious service in 1941. He was on duty when the ship struck a floating mine. The ship was struck amidships and water poured in. He was blown from the wheel stand. In spite of the injuries he had sustained and the shock he had received in the explosion he stuck to his post at the wheel and kept the ship straight. By his act extra time was gained to lower the lifeboats by which many lives were saved. He was one of the last to leave the sinking vessel.

ABDOOL ROHOMON x HAMID BUX (*E.R. Serang*)

Was awarded for distinguished service in 1942.

MURSHED MEAN x HYDER ALI (*Deck Serang*)

Awarded in 1942 for his distinguished service, i.e. for his personal example of coolness, courage and devotion to duty when the ship was dive-bombed by an enemy plane while at sea in 1941.

RUCKBOTHALI (*Deck Serang*)

Awarded for distinguished service.

ELLIE BUX x ZAFIR ALI (*Seacunny*)

Awarded 1943. See citation Captain Earl, O.B.E.

SHAHITULLAH x SK. ABUTH ALI (*Seacunny*)

The ship sailing in convoy was torpedoed and had to be abandoned. The survivors were picked up and no lives were lost. The Indian Quartermaster showed great courage and devotion to duty. He was at the wheel when the ship was hit and he remained at his post until orders for final abandonment were given. His excellent behaviour throughout set a good example to his fellow countrymen.

KOREME ALI x NAZEER ALI (*Seacunny*)

Awarded for meritorious service in 1944 when the vessel was attacked from the air and during the attack difficulty was experienced in manœuvring the ship, as she was well down by the head, having been hit when the attack was first made. In spite of the handicap the steersman managed to keep the enemy plane on the beam throughout the attack.

MUCKMAN PANCHIA (*Deck Serang*)

Awarded for brave conduct when encountering enemy submarines.

HABIBULLAH ALLIMUDDIN (*Oilman*)

Awarded in 1941. When the vessel was attacked by the enemy in March 1940 and sustained a direct hit through the engine-room skylight, one of the Junior Engineer Officers together with Habibullah were stationed at the cylinder covers. The bomb exploded between them, the Junior Engineer being blown across the engine-room. His leg was broken and he sustained severe facial injuries. Habibullah was also blown off his feet and injured, though not so seriously as the Junior Engineer. All the engine-room exit ladders had collapsed and although the engine-room was plunged in darkness owing to failure of the generator due to the explosion, Habibullah remained with the injured officer. He assisted him to the bottom platform and along the tunnel to the escape ladder and eventually to the poop deck where they both arrived about fifty minutes after the explosion.

ALBERT MEDAL

VALLA PEMA (*Lascar*)
JAIRAM NARRON (*Lascar*)
See citation N. E. Little (Albert Medal)

COMMENDED

JOHN ANGIER (*Purser*)
For good services in *Baroda.*
MOTIUR RAHMAN (s.s. *Erinpura*)
For good services in 1943 when the vessel was attacked by enemy aircraft.
BHOWEN METHOR (*Deck Serang*)
For good service in 1944 when the vessel was attacked by enemy aircraft.

LLOYD'S WAR MEDAL

K. S. SHAHABUDDIN (*Cadet*)
See citation (British Empire Medal)

4

SHIPS LOST

ENEMY ACTION

1. *SIRDHANA*	13th November 1939, *mine*
2. *DOMALA*	2nd March 1940, *bomb*
3. *MASHOBRA*	25th May 1940, *bomb*
4. *ASKA*	16th September 1940, *bomb*
5. *NOWSHERA*	18th November 1940, *raider*
6. *NALGORA*	2nd January 1941, *torpedo*
7. *GAIRSOPPA*	16th February 1941, *torpedo*
8. *NARDANA*	8th March 1941, *torpedo*
9. *HOMEFIELD*	2nd April 1941, *bomb*
10. *QUILOA*	15th April 1941, *bomb*
11. *GOALPARA*	15th April 1941, *bomb*
12. *JUNA* (H.M.S. *FIONA*)	18th April 1941, *bomb*
13. *BANKURA*	21st April 1941, *bomb*
14. *CHAKLA*	29th April 1941, *bomb*
15. *WINKFIELD*	19th May 1941, *mine*
16. *DEVON*	19th August 1941, *raider*
17. *CHAKDINA*	5th December 1941, *bomb*
18. *CHANTALA*	7th December 1941, *mine*
19. *CHILKA*	11th March 1942, *warship*
20. *GANDARA*	6th April 1942, *warship*
21. *MALDA*	6th April 1942, *warship*
22. *INDORA*	6th April 1942, *warship*

23. *FULTALA* — 7th April 1942, *torpedo*
24. *MUNDRA* — 6th July 1942, *torpedo*
25. *GARMULA* — 23rd July 1942, *torpedo*
26. *HATARANA* — 18th August 1942, *torpedo*
27. *HARESFIELD* — 9th September 1942, *torpedo*
28. *HATIMURA* — 3rd November 1942, *torpedo*
29. *KARANJA* — 12th November 1942, *bomb*
30. *CRANFIELD* — 23rd November 1942, *torpedo*
31. *TILAWA* — 23rd November 1942, *torpedo*
32. *NIRPURA* — 3rd March 1943, *torpedo*
33. *UMARIA* — 30th March 1943, *torpedo*
34. *GOGRA* — 2nd April 1943, *torpedo*
35. *WAROONGA* — 6th April 1943, *torpedo*
36. *NAGINA* — 30th April 1943, *torpedo*
37. *ERINPURA* — 1st May 1943, *bomb*
38. *GHARINDA* — 5th May 1943, *torpedo*
39. *DUMRA* — 5th June 1943, *torpedo*
40. *TALAMBA* — 10th July 1943, *bomb*
41. *WARFIELD* — 15th August 1943, *bomb*
42. *ROHNA* — 26th November 1943, *bomb*
43. *DUMANA* — 24th December 1943, *torpedo*
44. *SURADA* — 26th January 1944, *torpedo*
45. *NEURALIA* — 1st May 1945, *mine*
46. *SIR HARVEY ADAMSON* — 18th April 1947, *mine*

MARINE CASUALTY

47. *GOLCONDA* — 24th February 1940, *grounded*
48. *URLANA* — 5th September 1943, *grounded*
49. *SANTHIA* — 25th November 1943, *fire*
50. *BARODA* — 14th April 1944, *fire*

SUNK AS BLOCKSHIP

51. *GAMBHIRA* — 5th November 1939

INDEX

Index

Index

Index

Rail Post

Carvings on tops of rail posts at Buddha Gaya

Lithographed at the Govt. School of Art, Calcutta by K.C. Ghose Studio